READY, SET, INVEST

A High Achievers Guide to Private Real Estate Investing

DANIEL REILLY

ISBN Paperback: 979-8-89316-699-6
ISBN Hardback: 979-8-89316-680-4
ISBN eBook: 979-8-89316-698-9

DOWNLOAD THE AUDIOBOOK FREE!

To say thanks for purchasing my book, I would like to give you the Audiobook version 100% FREE!

I know you're more likely to finish this book if you have the audiobook. I even narrated the book myself so it will feel like we are having a conversation.

Instead of paying $10-$20 for the audiobook, I'd like you give it to you for free...

READYSETINVESTBOOK.COM/AUDIO

To Erin for always believing in me

No great thing is created suddenly.

—Epictetus

CONTENTS

Appendix

Introduction

"More of That"

Welcome to *Ready, Set, Invest: A High Achievers Guide to Private Real Estate Investing.*

This is a book about getting started and making progress. It's about doing big things. It's about making decisions. Informed decisions with a high degree of conviction. It's about leveling up and playing bigger. It's about thinking different. And about expecting different.

Fundamentally, it's a book about *doing what you would do if you weren't afraid.*

In fact, that question—"What would you do if you weren't afraid?"—is the single question that drove me to create this book in the first place.

An honest answer to this question might be the only thing standing between you and what you really want in life.

That's because, as quickly as your answer presents itself to this query, so does the realization that the only thing keeping you from what you really want is the story you are telling yourself. If you didn't have the fear, then you'd act differently.

And this acting differently would create different outcomes. Bigger outcomes. The outcomes you really desire.

The first time I was posed that question, nearly 20 years ago, I answered with the first thing that came to mind, stating bluntly: "I'd start my own business and invest in real estate."

Looking back, I think I picked that answer simply because those seemed like practical paths to financial success and the bigger life that I desired. However, from my vantage point, both paths involved some risk. Risk that I was apparently not up for at the time.

How about you? What would you do if you weren't afraid? And how would your life change as a result acting without fear?

Is there financial abundance? Freedom of time? Meaningful work with people you enjoy?

A High Achiever's Journey

Following through on my promise from the title, this book is for high achievers. It's also a guide that focuses on how to be successful with private investments (defined as investments created and managed by a private individual, as opposed to traditional public investments, like stocks and bonds, sold by an institution). That's because my attempt to do the things I would if I wasn't afraid led me on a journey of private investing that included starting a new business and acquiring investment properties.

The first big step I took on this journey was purchasing a single-family rental home in 2009. It required a huge amount of conviction as I was mocked and jeered by many of my peers at the time. They just couldn't make the connection between this ugly cinder block home in a working-class neighborhood of Jacksonville, Florida, and my dreams of financial independence.

A couple of years later, I owned five such homes and had issued several hard money loans to other investors buying similar properties. Both activities led to recurring passive income and a reduction in my reliance on the income I was earning in my job as a sales executive.

For the first time ever, I saw how life could function without a paycheck. I experienced how a couple of well-designed private investments could replace the need for a job or earned income. That ah-ha moment created confidence, and I felt comfortable moving towards the other activity on my original "what I would do if not afraid" list. So, I left my job as a highly paid employee to step into entrepreneurship and start my own company.

It turns out I had good reason to be fearful of launching my own business. That's because within 48 hours of filing for incorporation with the state, I was served a lawsuit by my former employer. They had a history of bullying sales guys that pursued other lines of work, especially anything they perceived to be competitive.

So instead of having a bank account full of cash to fund my first major investments as a business owner, I drained the whole thing within two weeks to defend myself and just keep the entity open. A few weeks of tense "lawyering up" led to them backing off, but the damage had been done. I was on my heels and questioning my decision before I booked the first sale.

I fought like hell to get that business off the ground and make it work. Recruiting our first customers and the employees to service them was challenging work. I had to pivot three times in the first two years since, you know … failure. "Pivot" is small business talk for "that didn't work, but we aren't giving up yet."

Fast-forward nine years, and I had managed to create a profitable enterprise that generated $15M in recurring revenues, served an important role for hundreds of customers, and eventually provided the financial abundance that motivates people to become entrepreneurs in the first place.

But then another issue popped up. I was miserable. *Miserable.* The opportunity to innovate had passed, and I was stuck doing things I didn't enjoy just to maintain a business and the lifestyle it provided for my family and me.

I'm sure you have no idea what I'm talking about when I reference feeling unhappy or stuck in your line of work. But if you can somehow stay with me on this, we can recognize that this happens quite often. Even to high performers who seem on the top of their game to the outside world!

Other Income

So after more than 15 years fighting the good fight each day as an employee, executive, and entrepreneur, my professional path again came to a crossroad. Something had to change.

That's when that question popped back up. "If you weren't afraid ..."

Yup, as uncomfortable as it was, it was time to face this query again. But this time, I wasn't a kid blurting out the first thing that came to mind. Instead, I spent months contemplating the question and recruiting mentors and trusted peers for feedback and help answering it.

I began to look back at the life-defining experiences I had been through and started to document what I had learned from them. I thought through the decisions that had turned out to be positive and profitable. I also relived some decisions that turned out to be failures and caused me lots of pain, stress, and loss.

This process of discovery culminated one night at the dinner table with my wife. We were reviewing some financial documents before I sent them to our CPA to calculate our taxes for the year. There was a lot going on—we had sold a personal home and some of the investment properties in addition to the business I was selling and our personal paychecks. She was asking great questions, seeking to understand the real impact of each of these sources on our family's wealth and prosperity.

At one point, her eyebrows raised, and she pointed to one line on the document:

"How do we do more of that?"

She was pointing to line 8 on the IRS form 1040, eloquently named "Other income." The reason she was focused on it was two-fold. First, it was hard to miss as it was the biggest number on the page and represented most of the total income that we had "made" as a family that year. And second, it wasn't very clear what we "did" to make it.

The rest of the form was self-explanatory. Line 1 was "Wages," and she understood that one very clearly as we both had been working hard to earn "W2 income" as employees for over a decade. Lines 2 through 7 were small amounts, so they were easy to ignore. But line 8 ... yeah, that one deserved some explaining. As we followed the trail of money, we learned that all of the "Other income" was composed of rents we had received from the properties we owned and the profits we made from selling some of them.

That was it. A vast majority of our wealth and income had come from a couple of homes located 2,000 miles away. "I've never even seen those properties." It was true. I had trusted partners in Jacksonville managing the units, and Erin had literally never laid eyes on them.

The conversation that followed was high energy and full of conviction. Erin had seen firsthand the toll that entrepreneurship had taken on me and our family. Well, at least the version of entrepreneurship I had been living.

The most important observation that came out that night was around how work impacted each of us. Erin shared that when I was talking about investment real estate, I lit up. It was fun. I smiled. The pitch of my voice went up. My eyes widened and my attention narrowed. "I think you'd do that stuff even if you didn't get paid," she concluded.

Meanwhile, my role as leader of a small business had been turbulent at best. Challenging customer relationships. Large, risky investments in inventory that didn't always pay off.

The constant recruitment of new talent, the development of current talent, and the removal of underperforming talent. Leading that business was a rollercoaster.

Erin shared that ultimately, "I just want you to be happy." And it seemed that certain attempts to earn income led to a naturally happy and energetic Dan while other pursuits led to a distracted, anxious, and sometimes pessimistic Dan. And now, we were learning that the light-hearted work might be more profitable than the hard-charging work?

So that became the challenge: make the acquisition and management of income-producing assets my main thing. It's a path that had huge opportunity for upside, a track record of success, and an activity that seemed best for my personal state and our family. If we had created most of our income from an activity my wife didn't even "see" happening, it's likely a good answer for exploring for the next stage.

An Investor's Journey

Over the next two years, as I will explain in detail in the pages to follow, that's exactly what I did—focused on making investment real estate a full-time pursuit. In the process, along with a business partner that I'll introduce shortly, we've acquired 897 units of commercial multi-family real estate with hundreds of additional units under contract or in our pipeline. To make that happen, we've created a community of 87 investors that have contributed over $24M of private capital to fund our acquisitions.

This journey has been rich with learning opportunities and lessons. In fact, I really haven't stopped the discovery process that started at the dinner table that night. This is a topic that fascinates me, and I know it fascinates lots of other people because lots of other people want to talk with me about it.

Which brings us full circle. I find myself having the same conversation over and over with like-minded people—high achievers with good jobs (or running healthy businesses) and ample income to support their lives, who aren't confident on how to deploy the capital (cash savings) they've learned to create.

These individuals often ask the same questions and have the same concerns. It turns out that private investing (or attempting to scale up and go bigger with private investments) is something that lots of people would do if they weren't afraid.

Yet, fear holds them back, and they instead blindly purchase shares of Tesla stock or second homes they hope will become profitable one day.

While I make no claim of having the single answer to wealth creation, I do claim to have a formula that worked for me and that is working for many peers, friends, and others that I have shared it with.

I've organized it in an embarrassingly simple framework that we all can follow. Regardless of where you are on your private investing journey—whether you have millions of dollars deployed or are anxiously waiting to commit the first meaningful chunk into a real estate or private business deal—the process I'm about to share is valid and worth looking at in totality.

Early in the process of documenting these lessons, I noticed the parallel between what I was learning and a simple 1-2-3 framework that all of us are accustomed to via the start of any big race.

Ready-Set-Invest Framework

Much like the cadence of the starter before releasing athletes via the starting gun, my process of becoming a private investor is as simple as Ready-Set-Invest. Let's go through how it's organized.

Starting with Part 1: Ready, I share my story on changing our fundamental beliefs about work, money, and investing. This includes a personal audit to understand why you're really doing this in the first place and some frameworks to help you think about how it is going to play out long term.

Then, in Part 2: Set, I show you how to develop an investment strategy that accomplishes your goals and massively reduces risk in the process. I share multiple strategies that I'm using to protect downsides, increase upsides, and stay aligned with your investments as they scale.

Finally, in Part 3: Invest, we get into the specifics of investing in commercial assets and setting those investments up for success. Private deals can seem intimidating and complex when they are new. After reading these chapters, many of the common questions will be cleared up and you'll feel ready to move forward on investments that are only available to the wealthiest individuals.

The 18 chapters that compose this book are each driven by a single idea, lesson, or tool I picked up over the past few years learning how this game really works. I'll admit it, I've become obsessed with learning everything I can and gaining an edge in the process.

The reality is that "acquiring income-producing assets" is an activity that takes place on an institutional scale. I'm interested in continuing to climb that ladder of larger and more complicated assets, but I recognize the potential sweet spot that this book focuses on. I was drawn to document this unique perspective as it captures exactly what you'd want to know if you were in a similar situation to me three to five years ago. The path to where I stand today would be a lot easier with the 18 ideas I'm about to present.

Each part of the book contains six chapters. My hope and intent are that these lessons will propel you through the process to move forward and confidently become a private investor. And importantly, lead you closer to the life you value most. You know, *the one you would live if you weren't afraid.*

PART 1 READY

"Ready" refers to the stage of the journey where we audit where we are and determine what we really want from our work and investments.

CHAPTER 1

Playing on a Bigger Stage

It was late on a Tuesday evening, nearing midnight. The "Dad Walk" had concluded over an hour earlier, yet the conversation continued with high energy. It was early December, and I remember it being a chilly evening, so much so that I balanced the tension of wanting to run inside to warm up and continuing what felt like a very important conversation.

This walk had become a weekly ritual. Five or six dads, most of whom had just recently moved into our neighborhood, would meet up around 8:30 pm and "get some steps in" after everyone had put their kids to bed. Many Tuesdays, we'd rack up 10,000-plus steps and wake up half the neighborhood as we circled the streets, talking and laughing about whatever topics surfaced between a bunch of forty-something working dads.

On this particular night, after the official walk was done and the group had dispersed, I was engaged in discussion with a friend named Greg. And that's when he said it. The phrase that got stuck in my head for the next few months and would literally change the direction of my life.

If I were in your shoes, I'd lock up a 100-unit deal and figure it out.

To which my response was "Wait—you'd do what?"

Let me back up a bit and set the stage here. This fateful evening was in 2021, during one of the tensest periods of my adult life. On the verge of completing a major midlife pivot, I was in the process of selling the company I'd founded nine years prior to my business partners and declaring myself a professional free agent. I was finally doing what some of my mentors had been nudging me to do for years: "Find an easier way." More on that in a moment.

While I was convinced this exit was the right decision, the specifics of what I was going to do next with my professional life were still unclear. I had ideas, lots of ideas, but there was no concrete plan. This uncertainty was okay, as I intended to take some time to reflect and process what the last decade of building a business had taught me. I had been "heads down" on my first big entrepreneurial venture for nearly a decade and was very proud of what I had built, but had also recently realized some costly mistakes I had made along the way.

The company I had built provided me with the financial abundance I had always aimed for, but it also came along with a demanding daily schedule, hyper competitive market, and some challenging relationships. As I'll explain in examples in later sections, the business I ran had headwinds that made it incompatible with the life I desired to live as its founder, owner, and leader.

As a result, for this next stage of life and work, I had two major goals. The first was to find a career path that allowed me to *be* the dad I desired to be—free to attend all my children's events, coach their sports teams, and eat dinner as a family every night. The second aim was to select a business model with the wind at its back, i.e., with inherent advantages, and one that allowed me to play this second half of my career on the biggest stage possible.

I had a strong sense that real estate investing would play a role since it had been a consistent side hustle for most of my adult life. However, I wasn't quite sure what that meant. I had acquired, managed, and eventually sold a portfolio of single-family rental homes out of state over the prior decade. That experience taught me that the real estate business had some special advantages that other businesses and investments do not. However, I was completely blind to the interworking of the commercial real estate industry or institutional-grade investment assets.

Accordingly, as I thought about my options moving forward, "real estate investing" simply meant more single-family homes. Or, as I wrote in my journal at the time, I could "go really big and take down a triplex in Costa Mesa." Acquiring a three-unit building in coastal California would likely be a great investment if purchased and managed well, and it seemed like the next natural step for a guy who had owned six individual rental properties to date.

This brings us back to that chilly Tuesday night in December, standing on the grass outside my house, an hour after the rest of the dads had returned to the warmth of their homes. It was there that I outlined, for the first time to anyone else, my plan to invest a big portion of the proceeds from the company sale into a triplex locally.

Greg listened patiently, and as I concluded my plan, I waited for his affirming response. Instead, he paused. I'll never forget what he said next. "Dan, that's awesome …, but if I were you and in your situation, I would lock up a 100-unit apartment building out of state and figure it out!"

Thinking back to that moment, what he said seemed so ridiculous I don't even think I heard it clearly. I had literally never considered that as an option. I'm a fairly sophisticated investor and well-read student of the financial markets, but had always assumed that big real estate firms like real estate investment trusts (REITs) owned all the big apartment communities with 100 units or more. I clearly expressed my disbelief and confusion in the moment as Greg continued to explain his plan in detail.

"The main reason to go big is the economies of scale. Think about it: if one person vacates your triplex, you are at 66% occupancy and likely have negative cash flow every month it's not fully occupied. In a 100-unit apartment, 33 units would need to be vacant at the same time to ever have 66% occupancy. An apartment building is a self-sustaining business. You'd simply need to raise the additional capital to complete the purchase."

To say that I was intrigued with what he had just said was an understatement. You know that emoji of the exploding head? Yeah—that was me.

For every question I had about the feasibility of such a plan, Greg had quick and reasonable answers. What he was describing wouldn't be easy to pull off, but it certainly seemed possible. Eventually, we both realized we had work the next morning and needed to split ways for the night. As a parting gift, Greg referred me to two books and a podcast that he thought would be particularly useful for me.

Over the next few days, I devoured every resource Greg had suggested. I was hooked. I had gone from having no idea large apartments were owned by individual investors to being 100% confident that I could pull off such a feat.

And then it hit me—was *this* what my mentors had been referring to all these years?

A Bigger Future

The phrase, "You could be playing on a bigger stage," had been said to me more times than I like to admit. As part of a peer coaching group for the 12 years prior, this was feedback I had received often from the leader of our group in response to my updates. Every 60 days or so, we'd meet as a group and everyone would take ten minutes to update the group on their business and family.

No matter how good or bad things seemed to be in my life at the time of the meeting, this group's feedback would come out of left field and surprise me. It took me over a decade to figure out what the heck everyone was saying, and it was this talk of apartment buildings that made it stick.

As I reflected on Greg's grandiose plan and this piercing peer feedback, I was able to reconcile the two voices. The reality was, for the past few years, I had been playing small. I had been on defense. The company I started had a rough start—nearly two years before we were cash flow positive. That was really trying on me and my young family.

I had managed to turn the business around through sheer determination and got it to a point where it was stabilized, profitable, and had leaders in place to manage much of the daily operations. This was a big win, but in hindsight, it had put me into a protective mode. I was much more worried about losing key customers and top-producing sales people to competitors than I was about being innovative or making a big impact on the community around me.

This headspace, combined with industry headwinds, meant growing my company felt like I was fighting with one arm tied behind my back and an anchor strapped to my foot. I had stopped thinking big because I was too worried about surviving.

This was in drastic conflict with some of my core beliefs and driving motivations—I'm here to expand and grow and keep climbing Maslow's hierarchy of needs. I'm going after abundance, options, and joy. I'm aiming for freedom. Many forms of freedom. All day. Every day.

And I know from years of self-experimentation that my relationship to my future has a major impact on my state of being in the present. As best-selling author Dan Sullivan teaches in his acclaimed Strategic Coach program:

The only way to make your present better is to make your future bigger.

I've spent much of my adult life aligned with this law. In a state where my vision of the future was outsized and totally inspiring. I've also spent periods of time, like the one I faced in 2021, where my future gets smaller and I start looking for safety and security rather than expansion and growth. I started noticing all the "problems" around me, and I put focus and energy into those. I would tell myself I was trying to fix those problems, but in reality, I was just giving them more energy to shrink my future even further.

This trend came to my attention via some escalating feedback from peers, mentors, and eventually, my wife, Erin. One Friday evening, while sipping a glass of wine on our porch and watching our kids play in the front yard, she informed me that I had, in fact, become quite challenging to live with. My frustration about the business was spilling over into my behavior at home and negatively affecting some personal relationships.

At a coffee the following week with my executive coach, Vance, that darn phrase showed up again. "A bigger stage." He was suggesting that my future could be much bigger than I was allowing and that my current environment was preventing me from expanding and moving to another level of scale and impact. He also agreed with Erin that I seemed distracted as a dad and likely out of alignment with my core values.

So it was clear something needed to change in my life. I would need to take courageous action. However, the immediate future did not look as simple as "escape." No, attempting to move away from something often just brings you closer to it. Instead, I needed something to move towards.

CHAPTER 2

The Path of Least Resistance

In his book, *$100M Offers*, business coach and author Alex Hormozi shares a story of a friend who was struggling in his entrepreneurial venture. The friend had an amazing offer and business model that enabled him to grow and gain market share consistently. His company expanded sales for years; then suddenly he couldn't seem to grow at all. He implemented new marketing campaigns and activity goals for his sales team—but nothing seemed to work.

Hormozi writes, "He shared with me that he just couldn't grow the business. And he kept looking at all these things. Finally, I was like, dude, *you're selling to newspapers*."

After a quick examination of his friend's business model, the real issue was obvious—his core customer and sales channel was newspapers, an industry that was experiencing a compounding decline in sales of 20% annually. The issue was not due to the entrepreneur's effort, nor his offer, nor his team's ability to close deals. The issue was that his target market was disappearing.

This story hit home for me as soon as I heard it. Although not as bad as the newspaper industry—my prior business was experiencing a similar fate. Since I graduated business school in 2005, I had been working in a really great niche servicing technology resellers. At the time, company networks of servers and laptops were a huge priority for businesses and the managed service provider (MSP) model emerged to service these needs. This boom in demand created thousands of new companies around the country. As a wholesaler of popular hardware products that were used in the most common solutions, the company where I began my career hit the market at a great time.

Fast-forward 15 years and the landscape was quite different. Instead of the MSP model minting new resellers that needed good hardware vendors, the cloud computing wave began to gain serious traction with enterprise customers. Consumers using Google Drive to store photos were little threat to my hardware distribution business, but when large banks and hospitals started putting full workloads onto cloud computing services, their need for hardware went from millions of dollars annually to almost zero.

This was bad news for thousands of MSPs, system integrators, and technology distributors. And it was a concerning trend for me. No matter how strong my customer relationships were, or how sharp my pricing was, or how fast I could deliver—the reality was that my core customer was disappearing. The rush of new companies stopped, and consolidation hit the industry as scale became the most important thing in the game to deliver cloud services. I looked around and saw competitors closing up shop, selling to larger firms, or shifting business models to focus on other areas of the technology ecosystem.

DANIEL REILLY

The takeaway here is that we can make the future harder the moment we pick a certain path. The opposite of this is true as well—that a different choice, strategy, or direction could make the future much easier.

Hard and Easy

A few months prior to the "I'd buy a 100-unit" conversation with Greg in 2021, I attended what has become an annual event for me. The coach I mentioned in the prior section, Vance, hosts a number of leadership retreats at his facility in the San Jacinto mountains each year. These are three-day gatherings of around 12 individuals that turn off their phones, embrace the cool mountain air, and practice what he calls "The Three Rs: Review, Renew, and Recommit."

There is some guided discussion along with individual exercises where we answer questions about our beliefs and values. It's an intense weekend—not exactly a day at the spa. The environment is beautiful, and accommodations are comfy, but Vance is there to change lives, not play host at a bed and breakfast. The meeting starts at 6pm on Friday, and you really don't take a breath until bed at 10pm. The mornings start with a hike at 7am, and Vance has you staring deep into your soul by noon. It's just under 48 total hours, and it often alters the course of the next year for each participant.

The retreat held in September 2021 would mark the ninth time I had attended. This, along with multiple group meetings with Vance each year, and it's safe to say the guy knows me pretty well. In fact, he's one of the few people on this earth that probably knows me better than I know myself.

12

He's worked with so many hard-charging entrepreneurs and doing-their-best young dads that no matter what topic I bring to him, or crisis I seem to find myself in—*he's seen it before.*

This perspective, combined with a high degree of trust and vulnerability that I share with Vance, provides him with frequent opportunities to point out blind spots in my life. So, on the Saturday night of the 2021 retreat, after we had all finished sharing our personal stories with the rest of the group, we ended the official session for the evening. There was an option to take a final evening walk (it's always a hike in Idyllwild) with the group or head to bed and get some sleep.

As the attendees moved to grab either their shoes or pillows, Vance approached me and put his hand on my shoulder. "Thanks for being fully here, Dan. I love how much you want to be successful and serve your family. My only wish for you is … well … that you find the courage to choose an easier path. Maybe that whole making-money thing doesn't have to be so hard."

A passing comment from the coach. A life-changing moment for the student.

This interaction and these words have become a true north on my journey forward, and it's a lesson we all must understand to be successful at investing our hard-earned capital or building serious wealth through real estate—

- *You could be playing on a bigger stage.*
- *Maybe it doesn't have to be so hard.*
- *Find the courage to choose an easier path.*

At the time, I remembered and reflected on a rule that a boss taught me years ago in my first job: "It's good that most people don't try to do really big things, Dan. That means there will be little competition up there, and you have a much better chance to succeed when you really go for it."

What a concept—play so big that it actually becomes easier.

Then I took a hard look inside. I came to the obvious conclusion that my professional path at that moment was not on track to ever experience the level of freedom I pursued. And the years of working in outside sales and owning a small business had taught me plenty about the freedoms I was looking for.

The Four Freedoms

Around the time I was encouraged to "find an easier path" for earning a living and building wealth, I came across an article by the author mentioned above, Dan Sullivan. It's titled "The 4 Freedoms That Motivate Successful Entrepreneurs." I was knee deep in my journey as an entrepreneur, and I was certainly looking for more motivation and success, so this title was click bait for me. It's a simple article, but its premise blew me away. "Yes—exactly! That's what I'm talking about!"

To summarize, Sullivan lays out his framework of expanding freedoms that support one another:

1. Freedom of Time—to spend your working life doing what you really enjoy doing
2. Freedom of Money—to generate unlimited amounts of money and abundance

3. Freedom of Relationship—to spend time working with people you enjoy and appreciate
4. Freedom of Purpose—to pursue work aligned with your fundamental values and ideals

The truth was that my entrepreneurial journey had provided a taste of each of these at different points in my career. There were moments when my schedule was free, the money was rolling, and I felt like I was pursuing meaningful work with great people.

But my experience of freedom oscillated with my sales team's performance, my company's net income, and the headlines in my industry. It was this inconsistency and resistance to a perpetual state of freedom that my wife was talking about on the porch that evening and what Vance was referring to in our meetings.

But how does one create a life of ever-expanding freedoms?

Learning to Leverage

Leverage, in the financial sense, is a fundamental concept that means applying a small amount of input to achieve a larger output. The layperson understands leverage to mean a loan—they can borrow funds from a bank to reduce the amount of money they bring at closing, therefore allowing them to purchase a larger property than they could afford if paying cash.

By all means, this is a great application of leverage. (We'll be covering the topic of debt and the strategies we recommend in great detail in Chapter 11.) But as an entrepreneur for nearly 20 years, I've learned leverage comes in so many other flavors.

This really hit home for me in 2016. That year, my company secured a contract with the single largest customer in the IT hardware industry. They had a niche need, and we had the perfect skill set and team to help them. After months of discussion, setup, and testing, we went live with a joint effort. The results were awesome. Due to the sheer size of this company's customer list and traffic to their website, sales orders stacked up quickly in the first week.

I was used to really fighting to win business. My customers were good, fair people—but they had options and kept vendors honest by running most projects by a couple of comparable sources. All of a sudden, when working with this national brand, customers didn't shop at all. We quoted a price and delivery date—they responded minutes later with an order confirmation. It was beautiful.

It was also somewhat confusing for my team. "What? No price checks or expedite requests? They just take our first quote and order?"

My business partner, who had led the effort to create this partnership smiled, saying, "Leverage, my friends."

This was a high-leverage situation because we *borrowed* the resources that led to quick and easy sales. The brand name, the customer list, the website, the order flow, the credit lines, the logistics infrastructure—all of this became "ours" for that portion of our business. Just like a loan for a home purchase, it helped us create large results with a relatively small initial investment.

A few months into this project, we stepped back and saw the leverage clearly in the numbers. We had "1.5 members of our internal team supporting this customer channel. At the time we had 14 employees, so this was 10% of our payroll but was accounting for 30% of sales and gross profits. "Leverage, my friends."

When it comes to creating financial freedom personally and becoming a world-class real estate investor, I figured out I would need to apply leverage in some very specific ways. In the next chapter, we'll explore the vision I created for an easier path to that bigger stage. Taking 20 years of research, observations, and experimentation, I've zeroed in on a high-leverage strategy to more freedom.

CHAPTER 3

A Vision Guides the Journey

In 1908, a young journalist was offered the opportunity of a lifetime—to spend the next 20 years studying the 500 most successful and influential people alive at that time. He was to interview these leading figures and record their thoughts, experiences, and beliefs. The sponsor of this project was Andrew Carnegie, then one of the richest men in the world. He believed that the formula for success could be identified and a philosophy developed that could help people achieve their personal and professional goals.

Carnegie chose Napoleon Hill as his man for the job, then provided him with the introductions he needed to access the most successful and wealthy individuals of the time. In 1928, right on schedule, Hill published his groundbreaking findings in an article titled "The Law of Success." Hill later created the book *Think and Grow Rich* from these ideas, and, despite being written nearly a century ago, this work still ranks among the top-selling books in the genre of personal development today.

This idea of studying others' success has always seemed like a no-brainer to me, so when I set my sights on bigger stages and easier paths, I also went to work studying those who have done it before. And here's some good news—as lofty as some of what I'm laying out may sound, *millions* of people have done it before.

Millions.

In fact, a bunch of people are doing it right now.

The essence of studying success is finding commonality. If we look at 500 successful people, what is something that 400 of them do? Is there anything that all 500 of them do?

Of course, finding something completely universal is rare. Routines, relationships, and worldviews were highly diversified among the group Napoleon Hill studied, and this is likely true within any group of "successful" individuals. But there were plenty of commonalities as well.

The principles that Hill was searching for and documented are intangible. They are composed of mental frameworks and ways of thinking. It is a list of beliefs that came up time and again with his successful subjects. In my own personal research, I set out to document a more tangible list. I was on a hunt for people around me who had work and professional pursuits that provided an abundance of the Four Freedoms.

The 100 Coffee Campaign

On January 1, 2022, I found myself waking up to a strange reality. For the first time in nine years, I was not working at the company I founded. The company still existed. The rest of the team showed up for duty, orders were placed, boxes were shipped. Yet, this massive piece of my identity was now no longer, well, mine.

I did thoroughly enjoy the idea that I didn't have to lead a sales team huddle or review inventory reports or forecast sales by account like I would normally do on the first of a month—but this was bittersweet. And although I relished the fact that I had some time on the calendar to rest and reflect, I also knew I wasn't going to sit still forever. So I created a simple activity goal for myself to get out of the house most days and stay connected.

Similar to Mr. Hill above, I decided I would invite 100 successful and influential people to coffee. No strings attached, just a friendly sit-down between two peers talking about life and work. I've always been a fan of an hourlong coffee with a friend or new connection. I love hearing other people's stories, and it's amazing the relationships and opportunities that can come from 60 minutes of authentic connection.

I used to squeeze a few of these in each month between sales calls. Now I could make a full-time job of it. At these meetings, I would inquire deeply about my counterpart's career. What did they like? What would they change if they could? What was most important to them?

After each meeting, just like Napoleon Hill, I would go home and document all I had just learned from them. Their wins and sources of strength. Their fears and biggest failures. And since I was attempting to get conviction about my professional and financial future, I made sure we discussed their relationship to earning, saving, and investing money.

I built a quick template for the notes and recorded over 100 of these interactions. As the notes accumulated, I realized I was sitting on a treasure that likely held some answers to the comments ringing in my head:

- *You could be playing on a bigger stage.*
- *Maybe it doesn't have to be so hard.*
- *Find the courage to choose an easier path.*

Common Answers

While reading and rereading many of the notes, patterns emerged and eventually I came to some conclusions. Here are some of the key lessons that stood out from my conversations about creating wealth and experiencing fulfillment through work.

First—there are endless ways to make money. You can do it by providing high-end professional services or selling pool toys. You can do it building new homes or repairing them after they get damaged. You can raise private equity to fund corporate mergers or you can screen print t-shirts for youth sports teams. It all works. Find a way to add value to a segment of customers, do it at scale and—*bang!*—you've got opportunity for serious income.

While I seriously think no income generation idea is impossible, I also know now more than ever that they are not created equally. Some business ideas definitely qualify as "easier" to execute than others. And some of them play "on a bigger stage" than others as well.

Second—some people *love* how they make money and some people *hate* how they make money. Some see their work as a realization of their highest calling in this life. Others see it as a life sentence of boredom, anxiety, and political hunger games. The craziest part is these two people often work in the same office and attend meetings in the same boardroom.

We'll dive deep into our relationship to work and generation of income in the next chapter. For now, we can simply notate that work, however you define it, has the potential to deliver personal fulfillment and joy to everyone, but very few of us ever experience this state or stay there very long.

Third—not everyone that earns tons of income becomes wealthy. High-income and high-net wealth are two very different things. Rich and wealthy are two very different things. Money and capital are two very different things. (We cover this in Chapter 9.)

No amount of earned income will make you wealthy; it's all about what you do with that money after it's earned. Long term, it's about what you *own*.

Fourth and finally—every single person I've had a conversation with about money has money problems. And all money problems can be put into two categories—those of abundance and those of scarcity. I'll share two examples to illustrate.

I met a fellow dad from my kids' school who had commission checks coming out of his ears as he pulled up in a new Mercedes G-wagon with a fresh Rolex on his wrist. He had incredible sales talent and was in a lucrative position selling high-ticket items. However, within minutes of starting our conversation, it was clear that he had not attained financial freedom and likely never would.

A few days later, I enjoyed lunch with a humble mid-level executive that drove an early-model Tesla because it came with an HOV sticker that allowed him to drive in the carpool lane by himself. I quickly realized he had passive income streams coming out of his ears, and his biggest money problem was finding good investments to put all the cash that kept showing up in his bank account each month.

The difference was startling, yet there was really only one thing that separated the two: *assets.*

Ownership and control of income-producing assets, to be exact.

The mid-level executive kept his job because he is a risk-averse dude that likes routine and doesn't mind corporate politics. He also started buying rental properties and funding private credit deals when he was 22 years old. Two decades of compounding returns at nearly 20% had done its thing, and he now made three times as much in passive income than he could maxing out his company's salary and bonus package.

The flashy sales guy would need to keep being flashy his whole life because his money went out as soon as it came in. Even though his business was tied to real estate, he didn't own any income-producing assets and had a list of beliefs and other priorities preventing that from happening. Again, everyone has money problems—it's just a matter of which kind. Experience tells me that problems of abundance are much preferred.

The Power of a Sketch

Earlier, I described the leadership retreat I attended with my coach. One of the rituals of this weekend is to spend 20 minutes on Sunday morning drawing a picture of your future. Vance sets out paper and markers, gives a moment of instruction, and lets you go. I've had the opportunity to draw nine of these pictures over the years. I've saved them all in a folder to remind myself of something significant: every single one of them has been realized in a major way.

The most startling was in 2018 when I drew a picture of a big office. This was a high-energy time at my business when we were growing our team and expanding our customer base as quickly as ever. The team was crammed into a tiny office, and moving to a larger facility seemed like the single most important thing in the world to me at that time. It meant achievement and it also meant momentum and a vote of confidence for our next five years.

So I drew a picture of my dream office. It had two sections: the back half was warehouse space full of shelves and shipping lines; the front half was office space full of desks in a sales floor and surrounded by executive offices. It was a rectangular shape with the main entry and lobby at the front and a roll-up door on the south-facing side. I drew some trees and grass around two sides of the building to give it some color.

Less than four months later, my partner and I signed a lease for a new, upgraded space to call home. It was half warehouse, half office. The building was rectangular in shape and had a main entrance on front and a roll-up door on the south-facing side. I bet you can guess where the executive offices were located and which sides of the building had landscaping.

The best part is I didn't even realize how close the reality was to fitting the image until well after move-in. It wasn't until a few weeks in when I was unpacking the last boxes that I re-discovered the drawing. I pulled it out and nearly dropped to my knees. As they say: careful what you wish for! That south-facing roll-up door became a security concern over time as it isolated our parking lot and invited some unwanted trespassers every now and then. Too bad a north-facing door wasn't in my drawing.

Crafting My New Vision

As I experienced with the new office and many other times since, setting a vivid vision is the single most powerful tool in my arsenal to take big dreams and turn them into realities. So by March 2022, fewer than 90 days past the effective date on the sale of my company, I wrote down a clear and inspiring vision for my next phase.

I described a future where my income was generated by investments in high-quality assets, likely real estate, that provided essential services to a large and hungry addressable market. I saw myself working with a few select, high-trust relationships on projects that gave me energy and created a positive impact on the community around me. I could see a clear image of myself working in my zone of genius, leaning heavily on the type of work I love to do and the results I enjoy creating.

I also saw a vision of myself as the best dad and husband I can be. Involved, supportive, patient, present. It's the person I saw myself being for the most important relationships in my life. And no matter what path forward I chose, the Four Freedoms needed to be front and center, so I could make decisions based on the filter of "What's best for my family?"

This is *what* I wanted. I remained open to the *how* and *who* and *when*, but I had established a future state that I was excited to move towards. So the vision was set, and it began to take root. Over the months that followed, with the help of some friends and surprise advisors, I developed conviction around this vision and began to truly believe that this was my future.

Now it was time to actually do it.

CHAPTER 4

The High Achievement Trap

Let's start with a thought experiment. Imagine you are a college student, a senior, weeks away from receiving that hard-earned diploma. And a bit like in the "The Christmas Carol," you are treated to a preview of your future. Rather than ghosts haunting you, this is a sage advisor, here to calmly explain the path ahead that has been taken by so many before you. They begin:

> "You start your career at an entry-level position and work really hard to prove yourself. You fall into or get assigned a niche type of work, creating a certain result—contracts signed, boxes shipped, dollars saved, whatever. You are motivated and ambitious, so you get really good at it. You get promoted and increase your earnings by doing more of this work and creating excellent results. You invest more into your skills and become a promising young talent."

So far so good! If someone told me this when I was twenty years old, I would have jumped on board. The sage continues:

"This cycle of achievement and advance-
ment continues for years, maybe decades.
Promotions and titles and executive compensation packages follow, until one day you rise
to such a level that your work is just not fun
anymore. The motivation and hunger that
comes with youth starts to wane, and you
begin to believe you don't really like doing
this after all. The politics or the pressure or
the monotony finally get to you. But now
you are really good at it and get paid a lot of
money to do it. There is no other work which
you could immediately be paid as much as
you make doing this. This is where all your
skills, experience, and relationships are."

Trouble is brewing. The 20-year-old me liked the growth
path, but I'm growing concerned about my future optionality,
and my freedoms are seeming to run thin. Finally, our sage
closes their story:

"While you were getting good at doing this
work and creating this result, you got married,
had children, and bought a home. You get
some time off from work each year, which you
use to try to relax and escape. Yet the vacations
become stressful too. Travel arrangements,
airplanes, hotel beds, cranky kids (and cranky
you) off their routines. Meanwhile, your work
stacks up while you are away, so you return
to a mountain of unresolved issues, which
stresses you out before you even get back.
You feel trapped. You are trapped. Your life

consumes a certain level of resources, and you have one way of earning income needed to support your family's life and lifestyle.

Changing your work essentially means moving from one company that does a thing to another company that does a similar thing. And your job will likely be to create that same result you are good at creating. Isn't that why you got hired in this role in the first place? To do the thing you are good at doing? The fact that you no longer love the thing is not really the concern of anyone else, because you keep doing it. And so, you keep doing it."

Welcome to the High Achievement Trap. Although a tad pessimistic, the story above is an entirely accurate description of the career arc for many of the highest-achieving people I know. It applies to professionals in business, law, medicine, and finance. It applies to actors, musicians, athletes, and military generals. I see these situations as natural phenomena of the modern world and byproducts in the technological age of specialization.

In fact, this is a strategy in corporate America. The term "golden handcuffs" is used to describe the compensation packages specifically designed to keep employees at a firm for the long term. The idea is to pay someone *just* enough to make them not leave and keep producing for the company. There are consulting firms that travel around the country teaching human resource departments at big companies how to implement these strategies into their management ranks. Young, promising stars are "locked up" by well-capitalized firms every day to ensure longer tenures in their current roles.

Golden handcuffs and the High Achievement Trap apply to many entrepreneurs as well. Rather than having a big firm ensnare them, they do it to themselves. Very few small business owners ever get out of the day-to-day operations of their company. Michael Gerber famously described this situation in his 1995 book *E-Myth: Why Most Small Businesses Don't Work* where he points out that most business owners work *in* their businesses, not *on* their businesses. And until that shift is made, the so-called "entrepreneur" is really a business owner that created a demanding job for themselves and is stuck.

Making this personal, the hypothetical story above was really easy for me to write ... because it's my story! And it fits the journey of Greg—that dad who I was walking with who challenged me to invest in those 100 units—as well. We went to different schools, got different degrees, and worked in totally different industries. We both even sought different paths to become business owners. I started a company while Greg pursued the partnership route of an established firm. Yet, at around 40 years old, we both found ourselves in the *exact* same spot—well-paid executives with equity and influence ... and completely trapped by the success that got us there.

Greg and I actually started calling this predicament the "Chapter One Problem" within a few months of starting our real estate business, Measured Capital, because of the conversations we kept having with peers. At the coffee meetings I was having on a daily basis, these feelings of being trapped by one's success kept coming up, over and over. Greg was hearing it too. One day, as the commitment to create this book began to take root, I said, "The first chapter will obviously describe this issue that everyone keeps pointing to." Greg, always ready to summarize my long-winded ideas, responded, "It's the Chapter One Problem!"

Clearly Not Trapped

There is another, brighter side to the High Achievement Trap—some people fall into a zone of high achievement and optimize their earning potential, but they also happen to love what they do. Call it luck or good planning—these folks started in the exact industry and career path that they still love decades later.

There are many great examples of this. One that stands out to me is Vin Scully of the Los Angeles Dodgers. He started calling the MLB franchise's games on radio broadcasts when he was 22 years old. He continued that effort until he was 89 years old. That's correct—67 straight years on the microphone. In the process, he also earned a massive salary and became a legitimate sports celebrity. However, that all seemed to be gravy for Vin. He just loved those Dodgers and wanted to spend his life watching professional baseball games from the press box.

Another example close to home is my dad. He graduated from college with a bachelor's in business. He then served in the Air Force as a pilot and an officer until returning to get a graduate degree in accounting. His first job was performing audits for government entities through a CPA firm in Orlando, Florida. Fifty years later, he is performing audits for government entities through a CPA firm in Orlando, Florida. His level of expertise, size of client list, and influence in the industry have grown significantly through his career. And the CPA firm now has his last name in the title.

But the outcome for which he gets paid has not changed since his first day on the job. His clients need audited financial statements that are fair and without material misstatement. That was the task back then, that is the task now. Today, at 80 years old, he continues to go into his office each day to move work files forward for his audit clients. He loves every second of it. I know this because I've watched it firsthand for 40 of those years. He's a volunteer at work!

He loves his routine—waking up around 5am, to the office by 7am, then home around 5pm to enjoy time and share a meal with my mom. On weekends, you'll catch him sneaking into his home office for an hour of focused work. On the side table by his bed, you'll find trade magazines for CPAs and forensic auditors. You know, for some causal pleasure reading. Multiple times a year, he travels to continuing education seminars around the state, both to learn and to speak. All of it gives him energy and fulfills a purpose in his soul. It also provides a healthy income that has grown through his career as he grew his name, credibility, and client list.

Regarding these high achievers who are earning a good living and love what they do—kudos! Literally, congratulations. I believe having work that feels meaningful and purposeful is one of the greatest gifts one can receive. For the rest of us, we're searching for a solution to this pesky Chapter One Problem and a way out of the trap.

You're Not Alone

Talented, educated, motivated, and purposeful individuals enter the professional ranks every year—and most of them end up in the trap. Under the surface of big salaries and big titles, many of the most accomplished professionals today feel stuck. They often work for big brands, manage big teams, and operate with big budgets, but have limited or no access to the Four Freedoms introduced in Part 1, so they continue to feel small.

In 2019, right as I was hitting a low in my relationship with the Chapter One Problem and the trap it sets, I was forwarded an article that shook me into action. Titled "Wealthy, Successful and Miserable," it is authored by best-selling author and Harvard Business School (HBS) graduate, Charles Duhigg. In the article, he describes attending the 15-year reunion of his HBS graduating class. To his surprise, as he discussed the careers of his classmates, he learned that many had risen to the top of their professions yet were miserable. Here's an excerpt from Duhigg's article:

> *There was a lingering sense of professional disappointment. They complained about jobs that were unfulfilling, tedious or just plain bad. One particular classmate described having to scramble to hit his daily goals while co-workers constantly undermined one another in search of the next promotion. It was insanely stressful work, done among people he didn't particularly like. He earned about $1.2M a year and hated going to the office.*

The article goes on to describe a moment when the individual in the example above considered another job he had been offered with a startup but paid half as much. His wife laughed at the idea, and he quickly calculated he couldn't support their current lifestyle with that pay cut.

Talk about being trapped! This individual is likely very talented and worked his tail off to get to his current position, yet was unaware of what life would look like once he got that big time job. High achievers can often be obsessive, so some of us forget to look up and figure out where our careers are going before we get so far up the ladder that we can't turn back.

Escaping the Trap

So what's the formula for escaping the High Achievement Trap once we find ourselves deep in one? The key is to turn our attention and focus towards something else. Something bigger.

As I will lay out in the chapters to follow, through all of my research and observation over the past 20 years of attempting to increase my freedoms—the one answer that keeps coming up to solve this dilemma is *assets*.

Ownership and control of income-producing assets, to be exact.

These assets come in a wide variety—some are physical like a piece of real estate. Some are intangible like a patented idea or copywritten music. For me, the path quickly narrowed to one of the purest examples of these assets: large, professionally managed, multifamily real estate. Also known as apartments. These properties are a straight path to passive income for investors and represent one of the best risk-adjusted returns of any method to deploy capital.

My hope is that my journey will provide a tangible example and show a clear path that you can follow to find an asset class that aligns with creating the kinds of freedoms you are going for. You might utilize commercial real estate to move out of the trap, or you could find another path more suited.

I cover the launch of Greg and my investment activity with Measured Capital in a later section. However, before you can launch, you have to be ready. (Remember? It's the title of this section.) To be ready, you first must define success for your path ahead.

CHAPTER 5

Defining Success and Rethinking Returns

In 2007, I realized a major life goal and simultaneously made the biggest investment decision of my life. Many of us have experienced this moment, also known as "purchasing my first home." It was an exciting time. I was engaged to my now wife, Erin, and my career had started off with a bang. I was experiencing the spoils of monthly bonuses at work as the team I had joined set sales records month after month. We have some great stories about making that house purchase happen, like putting 5% down and taking out two mortgages.

And because I live in the forever-high-demand real estate market of Southern California, we made a killing owning it, right?

Actually ... no. I held onto that house with white knuckles for nearly seven years and still lost money when we sold. That's because just a few months after we closed on this personal dream-come-true, it turned into a bit of a nightmare as the Great Financial Crisis came rolling through. As you may recall, home prices were destroyed in the months and years following the subprime mortgage crash and failure of the financial institution Lehman Brothers.

To be fair, I was an amateur that overpaid for a home that I'd bought highly charged by emotion and hubris. We were exceeding expectations at work, I was having fun and saw a very bright future ahead as I studied the guys that were a few years ahead of me. I was confident my earnings would continue to rise. And everyone at the office told me that residential real estate in the area was a sure thing. I'd likely see appreciation in the first few years, sell it for a big profit, and use that to upgrade to a larger home. This is exactly what had occurred to anyone I talked to that owned their home in the area.

That would not prove to be my fate. Instead, a once-in-a-generation crisis hit the financial markets a few months after I signed the deed, and soon, I owed way more on the home than it was worth. What had planned to be a two- to three-year stop became a seven-year lockdown due to restrictions on the loans I had taken out.

As frustrating and concerning as this situation was in the moment, looking back, I'm absolutely grateful that it occurred. It taught me some huge lessons about markets, timing, debt, real estate, capital, liquidity, and the mental side of buying big assets. I developed quite a bit of internal fortitude while forking over payments for years on an overpriced mortgage that I couldn't get out of. Most importantly, it caused me to pursue other strategies in real estate to offset this bad buy and the mortgage that was tied to it.

One strategy I found was out-of-state single-family rental (SFR) homes. At the time, the term "SFR" did not exist as we know it today. Single-family homes were still a "mom and pop" game and did not have many large-scale operators or institutional capital like there is today. In fact, it is the Great Financial Crisis itself that created single-family rentals as an official investing asset class because of all the foreclosures and amazing buying opportunities that it created for savvy investors at the time.

Eyes Wide Open

As the real estate markets melted down around me and I realized how stuck I was in terms of my options to refinance or sell out of this home, I began noticing that many of my peers and friends had started purchasing homes. And a lot of them were people that had not been in a position to purchase a home in California 12 months earlier. We were all just too young and the home prices too great.

But then it became apparent—not only were the home prices down 30% or more in many local markets, but interest rates on 30-year fixed mortgages were in the 3% range, meaning the monthly payment had dropped by more than half. This led to a surge in new home buyers who scooped up some of the best deals in the last century. Unfortunately for me, to purchase a new home would mean I needed to sell the one I owned, which would have represented a loss of nearly $200k. This was way more money than I could comprehend losing on a home I had lived in for a year, not to mention more than I could afford since that was more than I earned annually at the time.

So I started searching for other ways to take advantage of the discounted pricing and financing terms. Looking around my local area didn't make sense—the prices were still prohibitive in terms of investment properties. However, being from Florida, I knew home prices were much more reasonable there. So the next time I went back to see friends and family in Jacksonville, Florida, I made sure to block off some time to look at some real estate.

And what do you know? In 2009, like many markets at the time, the place was on fire sale. There were high-quality homes on the market for less than $100k. Distressed properties were selling for $60k. And if you had some relationships with the right people at the right bank who needed to unload large batches of them, a home could be purchased for $20k or less.

That's right, less than 15 years ago, people were buying houses in major Florida markets for less than $20k. Of course, these properties were likely squatted in for months prior to being foreclosed, taken by the bank, and sold to the investor. This meant some additional capital was needed to repair and make them rentable. But that still meant we had move-in-ready three-bedroom homes in decent neighborhoods for less than $50k. *In 2009.*

That's when I was introduced to the concept of price-to-rent ratio.

Price-to-Rent Ratio

While on my visit to Jacksonville, I made sure to meet up with a couple of friends that had been focusing on the local real estate market. In fact, they had been trying their hand at investing in a few properties—with mixed results. But they believed strongly that they were on to something and had some ideas as to how we could partner together to purchase properties. Before I was interested in doing a deal, I first wanted to better understand the numbers. How much exactly can we profit from the purchase of a home? Is it better to flip it or hold it and rent it out long term for cash flow? How much can a $50k home cash flow in the first place?

I sat down with the three founders of JWB Real Estate, who had been long-term friends and went through the mechanics of the deals they were doing. Knowing that I was fresh off the plane from California and frustrated with the high prices on entry-level homes there, they made sure to focus on the concept of price-to-rent ratios. This is simply how much the price of a home compares to how much it rents for. In 2009, and still today, this ratio is poor in all California markets—to the point where investors generally do not cash flow from SFR investments unless they put down a very large down payment.

In Florida, however, and many other markets in the country, there was a very favorable ratio. When the asking price was below $100k, the rents for a similar home were at or above $1,000 a month. As we'll discuss later, a cost basis like this has potential to generate a highly profitable investment if managed correctly. I didn't know it at the time, but this exact ratio describes something called the One Percent Rule in apartment investing and is a key metric used by many when evaluating deals today.

Focused on Cash Flow

When it came to actually breaking out a spreadsheet and doing analysis on those first few SFR opportunities, almost all of my attention was focused on cash flow calculations. More than anything else, my motivation for buying those SFRs was to create some kind of positive monthly number, knowing that I was getting huge benefits in other departments like tax savings, principal pay down, and long-term asset appreciation.

In fact, I typed the term "return on investment" (ROI) on the top line of those spreadsheets in big bold letters. Next to it was a number I calculated using a formula that I now know to be called "cash-on-cash return." Today, we use internal rate of return as our primary ROI metric as this is more common in commercial real estate and considers all of the financial effects of the investments over time. But the point is that, at that time, I was defining the success of that investment entirely on its operational cash flow. Any profits made from eventually reselling it later were pure gravy and not part of my analysis.

At the time, as a 25-year-old licking some early real estate wounds and trying to recover, the idea of purchasing an asset like this and not receiving monthly income from operations seemed ludicrous. In fact, it still seems ludicrous and that belief continues to feed our investing philosophy and acquisition strategy. More on that in the next chapter.

Regarding the homes I was considering in 2009, my calculations said I would be able to keep $300 of that $1,000-rent payment after all expenses and loans were paid each month. Additionally, the mortgages available at the time covered

80% of the purchase price by default. As we'll calculate in a moment, that combo creates an amazing return on invested capital. Numbers like this are hard to replicate given the competitive state of investment real estate today.

Recalling this story of evaluating my first investment in real estate reminds me of the crude method of analysis I used at the time. Yet, while simple, it also proved to be effective and accurate for the situation. It was a single door, with a single rent payment, and a single mortgage with very predictable annual expenses. So a simple formula like "income minus expenses equals profit" worked just fine. I did it on a single page, and it was easy to understand. Of course, bigger and more complex deals deserve bigger and more complex tools and analysis. We'll explore the most useful and commonly used measurements of return in the Appendix.

Valuing the Intangibles

In addition to learning some early and effective methods of deal analysis, this experience of making the decision to invest had another side benefit that might be worth more than all the financial returns that these assets delivered—the education and momentum provided for me to increase my game and play at a bigger scale.

In reality, investing is a mental and emotional game. As much as we try to make it purely objective, the decision to place six figures of capital into an investment with no guarantee of success or even return of that capital requires some subjective reasoning. The fear of failing as well as "analysis paralysis" is what keeps most individuals from ever getting in the game. There is so much unknown, it takes some faith at this juncture.

After a few months of owning that first rental, I got a view into the inner workings of leasing, tenant screening, collections, and maintenance. This taught me a few things I had not considered, and I added those wrinkles to my deal analysis spreadsheet. This iterative process continued with every acquisition as each new home and the experience of owning it made me a savvier buyer for the next one.

I gained confidence and built a track record. Future deals required less "blind faith" because I understood the mechanics and how to mitigate risks. Each deal became easier as I became a more educated and experienced investor.

There is actually a term for this—"The Law of the First Deal"—which can be attributed to Michael Blank and the education platform he has built around it. The premise is simple: getting a first deal under your belt—regardless of its size or form—is the priority because it starts the journey.

After the first deal is done, brokers and agents will take you seriously since they can see you are active and capable of closing. Banks will be quicker to approve your file when they see you're paying other loans on time. Other investors, peers, friends, and neighbors will ask about the investment and how it's going. Some of them will want to get involved and replicate your success or support you in doing more.

A first deal creates serious momentum and can change the direction of an investor's career and, for that matter, their life. I can attest to this being 100% true.

So as we move into the first truly technical topic of this book, let's make sure to put proper value on the intangibles. I was very fortunate and received a handsome financial reward for my early SFR purchases. Then again, the learning really started when I bought that first home in Orange County and got my butt handed to me by the market.

The big takeaway here: the real learning starts after you get into a deal, and by being intentional about your first investment, you can avoid some painful mistakes.

Common Return Metrics

Now that we've acknowledged the intangibles, I'd like to introduce you to the most common and effective methods of "advanced" deal analysis. Due to the technical nature of this topic, I've created an Appendix that covers every major return metric that I consider in my deals and that I suggest you get comfortable with. Investors often report being frustrated by large assortments of metrics used to express the anticipated performance of an asset—many of which they have never heard of before. It can feel like a foreign language and be very intimidating, even to savvy entrepreneurs and business executives. Get ahead of that obstacle now by getting educated on each of these and decide which ones will be most important to you moving forward.

It's important to state here that there is not a single source of truth for what makes a "good" investment. If there was and everyone agreed, we wouldn't have a need for the library of metrics that exist and are used by investors every day.

Instead, we must find the metrics that are most important to us individually and that support our unique goals and vision.

Defining Success

To close out this topic, allow me to share a simple observation—success is not the same for everyone, and it will evolve over time. The biggest mistake I see investors making is following someone else's definition of success, and never doing the hard internal work to figure out what really matters to them and what goals would truly support attaining it.

Using the tools I introduced earlier—playing big, choosing an optimal path, creating an inspired vision—you can define success on your own terms. Maybe you are aiming for the Four Freedoms like me. Or maybe you've discovered a "why" that is even more compelling to you.

Next up, in Chapter 6, we take a deeper look into our preferred asset class and discuss the rationale for it becoming the foundation of Greg and my investment business. Now that you have the tools to define success on your own terms, you might decide it's a good fit for yours as well.

CHAPTER 6

It's a Business AND It's Real Estate

So why commercial real estate again?

Couldn't I have invested in stocks and bonds? Traded options? Purchased tax liens?

Why not look at purchasing an operating business? Laundromats, car washes, and pet care services are all the rage; how about buying one of those?

Or software as a service (SaaS)? Nothing grows faster or sells at bigger multiples right now than niche software.

The real answer to why I developed so much conviction is because ...

> Commercial multifamily real estate is a business AND it's real estate. You get the best of both worlds, which reduces risk.

Truth is, all of the above methods can work. All of these methods do work ... for someone. But many of them require that someone to be uniquely skilled and very active. That would make those other methods a poor choice for me since I'm focusing on playing big and increasing the probability of being successful. Because I'd say it's a fair bet that you want the same, let me explain.

It's that probability of success thing that we'll focus on here. After all the observing and discussing and reading and experimenting, my conclusion is that large multifamily is objectively the best asset class. And although I've always heard that "most wealthy people get there through real estate," I wanted a more detailed answer. While deep in the data around this topic, I was introduced to a concept that forever changed how I look at investment assets—risk-adjusted returns.

The Sharpe Ratio

Back on that chilly night in 2021, it was Greg's "'100-unit deal" vision that got the wheels turning in my head. And the reason he had so much conviction in this plan was because of a risk measurement tool that he had learned about earlier that year. It was this tool that gave him the confidence to invest his first $50,000 into a multifamily syndication, which was a 150-unit community in Austin, Texas.

Greg originally discovered the sponsor of this deal (37th Parallel Properties) due to some great educational content and research they were publishing at the time. One of the pieces that stood out to him is titled "Commercial Multifamily Real Estate Is Significantly Less Risky Than the Stock Market." Due to some key points, it immediately became an important piece of my developing thesis as well. And it was the first time either of us had heard of the concept of the Sharpe ratio, a way of measuring investments for risk.

By looking at the volatility of an investment class and comparing that to its opportunity for returns over a given timeline, the Sharpe ratio measures how much risk the investor must take on in order to get the desired return. And the data has been clear for over 50 years—over any long-term period, commercial multifamily has the best Sharpe ratio of any investment class. In fact, all commercial real estate types rank higher on this scale than bonds, stocks, and private equity alternatives.

Reading this and reviewing the math was fascinating.

As I did, I realized I had just learned this lesson of "asset class risk" directly. In the two years leading up to this, I engaged in three seemingly unconnected transactions—selling my personal home, cashing out on some investment real estate, and exiting the business I had founded. Each sale was done for its own reason, and each had different dynamics. Looking back at these—they provide a real-world example of how the Sharpe Ratio plays out among different assets.

Terminal Values

When thinking about the risk of holding any particular asset, one of the biggest considerations is "how quickly can I turn it into cash?" That basic economic concept is called "liquidity" and something most new investors miss. Many are so enamored with the immediate returns that they forget to consider if they'll ever be able to offload what they've acquired. After reviewing the stories in this section, you'll have a great appreciation for the concept of "terminal value" (another term for "sale price"), and you won't make that mistake.

The first example is the portfolio of rental homes I sold in Jacksonville that I built up in partnership with JWB Real Estate. After gaining confidence through my first investment described in the prior chapter, I continued to purchase one new property every time I had enough cash to afford the down payment. By the time I was ready to sell in late 2019, I had a total of five homes.

Each of them had great financials. They rented for above $1,000 per month and cost about half of that to operate and finance, which created a history of profitable operations that could be proven via financial statements and tax returns. This meant they could be valued, or assigned a terminal value, based on their income. The buyer pool, which would consist of investors looking for income, would apply a cap rate (defined in the Appendix) to the net income of each property and arrive at a reasonable price.

Stating the obvious, these homes were also real estate. Meaning each could also be sold as a personal residence to a retail home buyer instead of other investors. In this case, they would be valued via the "comparable sale method" that is so prevalent in residential real estate. Any given home is valued based on what the neighboring homes are selling for.

My next example took place about a year later and taught me that homes can sell in 24 hours, all cash, for well above the asking price via a buying frenzy. In this case, we were in a market freaking out about COVID-19 and the need for more living space. We had a home with a big backyard and in walking distance to nature trails overlooking the water. It appealed to a massive audience of hungry and capable buyers. If this had been the only residence I had ever sold, I would have thought it was always this easy.

But my experience with our first home from 2007 to 2013 taught the opposite—some homes take years to sell. In that instance, we purchased the house at the peak, and it was financed with an inflexible mortgage. Instead of a buying frenzy, we got crickets from a buyer pool with better options. This was a long and painful process that ended with my wife and me actually contributing money at the closing table as we owed the bank more than we received in sale price.

The point of this is to say: you have no control over how the market views and values any particular piece of residential real estate at any given time. It will go up and down like the stock market, based on the levels of fear and greed prevailing at the moment.

Okay, our last example of an asset sale is unique because this one is not real estate at all. Instead, this is the operating company that I founded in 2013 and sold at the end of 2021. At the time of exit, we had $15M in revenue and the strongest profit margins of any company in our industry. Since this was clearly an income-producing asset, it was valued via the income method, similar to rental real estate held for investment.

Except in this case, there really is no "market value" or "comparable sale." That's because each small business is so unique and carries so many unique risks. The value proposition, the customer base, the internal systems and team that make it work—all of this may look great today, but it can falter quickly. Many businesses require expertise to operate.

Additionally, there are very few buyers for niche small businesses. That's bad for their terminal value. In fact, it's the number one problem with selling niche companies. If there are only two or three parties that even qualify to buy it, you'll have a tough time creating a bidding war at the time of your choosing.

Of course, some entrepreneurs are able to dominate a niche or be first to a market and sell their companies for crazy multiples and exit values. I'll let you in on a little secret—those examples are extreme outliers. A vast majority of businesses that sell each year are valued at two or three times their annual earnings … often less.

Two Floors

The takeaway from these direct examples from my recent past is that investment real estate mitigates risk by establishing two floors—one from an income valuation and one from a market comparable valuation. This provides protection of capital and reduction in overall risk.

Summarizing the above:

1. A single-family home is sold as real estate, with its value determined by the local market for comparable properties.
2. A small business is sold as a business, with its value determined by the ability to generate future income.

3. A rental property, like a portfolio of SFRs or an apartment complex, can be sold as either, with its value determined by the higher of the two.

This dual purpose, or "optionality," as I like to call it, of rental real estate—in this case the portfolio of five SFRs—was the deciding factor for me to choose it for the path ahead. It has the impact of providing two tailwinds to the asset—one for the business operations and monthly profits it generates and the other for general utility and market value of real property. This creates two floors on its value and price.

Still Standing

Considering the outcome of these examples brings us back to where we started this chapter—my conclusion that commercial multifamily real estate is objectively the best asset class to accomplish many investing goals. The market data and my anecdotes collaborate to support the idea that it provides the best risk-adjusted returns of any asset considered.

Here's a fun fact—100% of the apartments that were built in 2012 are still standing today. (Okay, a few of them might have burnt down or something crazy like that, but still, that would put it at around 99%.) And a vast majority are fully occupied and kicking off some serious income for their owners.

Compare that to the 25% of all businesses that were founded in 2012 that still exist today. That's a 75% failure rate and equates to a lot of money and effort spent to build things that no longer exist. Another data point to drive this home: the long-term foreclosure rate of commercial grade loans attached to large multifamily assets is below 1%. That equates to a less than 1% failure rate of the owner managing the asset. In nearly all of these cases, the foreclosed asset is sold to another buyer who quickly realizes its latent potential.

As great as all of this is, it's also a bit boring. Some investors want speed, novelty, and risk. There is plenty of room for crypto and AI startups over the next decade if that is your taste. And there is nothing wrong with that as long as it matches up with your primary goals and vision.

For me, and many others with a taste for passive income and expanding freedoms, multifamily is a slow and steady route that has the odds in its favor. Now it's up to you to take these concepts and apply them to your own journey toward becoming a professional investor.

These last six chapters have been all about the internal and mental side of investing. We started here because it's the necessary foundation to enable success. As we move to the next section, we advance the conversation into the actual strategies you can use to increase your chances of success as a private investor.

PART 2 SET

"Set" is the stage in the journey where we chart our path forward and find the easier path to exit the High Achievement Trap.

CHAPTER 7

Less Is More: The Magic of Constraints

Shortly after purchasing my first home in 2007, I also made some big moves at work. Well, that might be more accurately stated as "I had big moves made on me." After finishing my graduate degree in accounting from the University of Southern California, I made a hard left turn and took a position on the sales floor of a young company based out of Laguna Beach brokering computer parts.

After making some new friends during my time at USC, I got a surprise offer to join their company. Given that they had just won "Fastest-Growing Company in America" by Entrepreneur Magazine, it felt like a rare opportunity, and it looked like these people were having as much fun as you could working. My first 1.5 years were intense. I was assisting the top producer on the sales floor. My job was to make his orders ship and his customers happy. He also happened to be doubling and tripling the sales of the nearest competitor on our sales floor most months. It was fast-paced and demanding work that required constant problem solving throughout a ten-plus hour day.

I thought everything was hunky-dory until one day I got pulled into a room with the CEO. He informed me that, although the team performance was stellar, there were personality issues brewing on the sales floor, and he wanted to break our team up. This boiled down to two options for me: (1) move into outside sales and a fully commission-based income or (2) be terminated.

I took the obvious choice and stayed employed. And upon arriving at the office the next day, my desk had been moved to the other side of the floor, and I was officially an account executive. Except that I had zero accounts and near zero experience being an executive. I certainly had never managed a book of customers, nor had I built one. I was a fish out of water, to say the least. However, like most periods of adversity, it was among the best learning opportunities I've ever experienced. It was hard, and I struggled. Along the way, I had a couple of great mentors at the company that looked after me. They recognized how little I knew about the job I had just been granted yet also saw my potential and ambition to figure it out.

As this personal transition was happening, the company was bursting at the seams. We moved from an old retail center on the Pacific Coast Highway with ocean views to a massive automated distribution facility close to highways and local transportation hubs. The owners of the business also began to bring in middle management to look after young bucks like me.

When the sales manager—let's call him John—started, we sat down and reviewed my process. I shared that I was making hundreds of outbound calls every week to a list of prospects. John asked for that list of prospects, and I provided it. He asked me what was common about the companies on the list. I responded that they all sold technology solutions using HPE products.

"Good start, what else?"

Well, that was it. That was about as far as I had taken it.

His eyebrows raised. "Location? Size? Vertical? Nothing?"

I didn't even know what a "customer vertical" was at that time. He wasn't mad, but he saw the opportunity to teach via one of his famous stories. This guy was ex-Special Forces and gave me the first of many analogies that mixed some form of violence with sales philosophy: "Prospecting for new customers is like hunting," he explained. "Do you want to hunt with a shotgun or a sniper rifle?"

John was clearly a sniper rifle guy, and this proved to be the correct answer. He referred to the shotgun option as "spraying and praying" and felt firmly that it was not an effective battle strategy. Instead, the sniper has discipline and focus. By specializing in a niche, I could gain familiarity and expertise. He suggested that I pick two customer subsets and then remove every company on my list that didn't fit. This meant I was giving up on 80% of prospects I had been calling on. He promised me that opening up that space and filling it with highly focused effort would pay out exponentially over time.

At this point, I had nothing to lose. I had never sold before, and I had zero sales training. This guy seemed like he knew what he was doing, and from what I could see, he genuinely wanted to help me be successful. So I followed his plan and eliminated everyone on my list that wasn't an e-commerce marketplace or consultant specializing in virtualization software. I chose these niches because I saw them as "blue oceans"—markets that weren't "red" with competitors. I worked on a very aggressive sales team, and they had been turning over a list of prospects for years by the time I got my shot. Rather than calling on the same old list, I figured I'd go to emerging markets and try to get a first-mover advantage.

This decision to purposefully constrain myself turned out to be the single best thing I did as an employee of that company. I ended up developing a brand-new sales channel via the then unknown e-commerce space. After a few months, I teamed up with one of the company's executives, and together we opened the largest account in the space.

It was glorious. After being mocked by some of my peers for months as I pursued this new niche that had no proven history, they began asking very different questions once that big customer's orders started to ship and my sales volume nearly doubled overnight.

Turns out, I'm not the only one to have figured out the magic of constraints and focus.

The One Thing

The nationwide real estate agency Keller Williams got its start in 1983 out of a single office in Austin, Texas. Within five years, they began franchising the model to other cities. In the 1990s, the company experienced exponential growth in their number of offices, agents, and home sales. The firm currently employs 180,000 agents and clears hundreds of billions of sales volume each year.

One of its co-founders, Gary Keller, has shared many of the principles and strategies behind the company's growth in his book *The One Thing*. The message of the book is to extoll the power of focusing on one thing to achieve extraordinary results. He believes strongly that his company's continued growth is due to the fact that it's the single thing he always focused on. The quote from the book that stands out to me in summarizing how to implement this strategy:

> *What is the one thing you can do so that by doing it, everything else would be easier or unnecessary?*

Although this book had not yet been published when I was learning the sniper versus shotgun framework, I discovered the principle at the perfect time. Years later, I found myself in a sales slump and couldn't figure out what I was doing wrong. In hindsight, I was trying to get cute and had become distracted with lots of little things that didn't drive the core result. A mentor saw this and suggested Gary's idea and book. After a few chapters, I got the message and quickly shifted my activity back to the one thing I knew drove results and blocked out everything else.

Constraints Keep the Focus

The application of this concept to investing in real estate is simple—hunt for opportunities with a sniper rifle, not a shotgun. This means understanding our one thing, so we can install "constraints" into our process and develop criteria.

Otherwise, we are just "spraying and praying." It also means developing an opinion and a conviction in that opinion.

Real estate investors and the brokers that help sell real estate investment assets often refer to this set of constraints as a "buy box." It has criteria, also known as "constraints" on all sides—location, price, type, size, class, etc. After a year of being active in multifamily real estate investments, Greg and I added more constraints to our buy box, such as required vintage (age of the building) and eliminating a few sub markets within our target MSAs due to highly localized trends that we became aware of by being active in the market.

Without constraints and the discipline to stay within them over time, investors can get pulled in many directions. I've seen many individuals tell me in depth why they love apartments and are committing to them—only to see them buy a hotel or retail center six months later. This is how some investors get in the game to pick up assets, only to find that they acquired some liabilities due to a lack of focus and scattered activity.

Accordingly, my goal was to become a master of one slice of the commercial real estate game. Looking back, I believe that was a great move and one I would recommend to anyone going down this path. Find a specific niche within a given asset class and go deep to gain expertise and mastery. Later, in Chapter 9, I will go over how to develop an investment thesis and the constraints that come with it. Before we get to that, we have an important step to complete—committing to the work.

CHAPTER 8

Chop Wood, Carry Water

There is a Zen proverb that I often recall to myself anytime my work starts to feel overwhelming:

> *Before enlightenment, chop wood, carry water; after enlightenment, chop wood, carry water."*

This phrase summarizes a truth about the human experience—no matter how high we climb or how big of a stage we play on, there will always be work. For anyone striving for mastery or success in any field, they must remember that the path ahead is filled with decades of daily effort. This is not bad news. Well, it might be if you find yourself dealing with the Chapter One Problem and are stuck in a High Achievement Trap.

For me, it offered inspiration to make the changes in my environment and my beliefs to find joy and fulfillment during a "routine day." One great part of modern life is that we can shape what that work looks like. I know that I get fired up when I meet with members of my community and get to talk about real estate investing. I also like reviewing financial statements and underwriting models (not preparing them), building operating budgets and business plans, and spending time on-site at properties with an eye for opportunity. I also like to write and publish my take on certain topics. Each of these is serious work that adds serious value to Measured Capital.

For me, these are all "get-tos." I would likely do them even if I wasn't getting paid. I intrinsically enjoy the action involved. Take financial statements, for example—a balance sheet and income statement are a total mystery to most people. Many executives don't really know what they are looking at or the story being told through a company balance sheet. However, I studied financial reporting at the graduate level and truly enjoy reading financial statements and talking to the people that prepared them. I like investigating sub accounts to see the transactions and ensure they are being classified fairly and in alignment with reporting and tax requirements. Other people find this activity total drudgery.

Meanwhile, spending hours of my day in blocks of outbound cold calling is a surefire way to kill my energy and motivation. I did it for over a decade but forced every minute. I have a friend that used to work with me at the technology company and still sells high-ticket contracts today. She loves the telephone. It's her "get-to," and she's insanely valuable when she's on a call block. Want to get a meeting with the CEO of a dream prospect? Give her three months and a good reason; that meeting is gonna happen.

If you gave me that goal, I'd do everything I could to hack it and find a way around the system. She would burst through the front door with a cup of hot coffee and be undeterred if the CEO refused to see her on a surprise visit. Then again, she'd tactfully show up the next day and eventually the meeting would be granted.

Chop wood, carry water. I will be doing some version of work for the rest of my life. I want to make it easy on myself and pick work that I actually like. Remember that meaningful work is different from the pleasure one gets from leisure activities. I, too, would rather be sitting on a beach in Hawaii than at a desk reviewing financial statements. But the Hawaii gig doesn't exactly pay very well. I'll be honest and admit that, much like my dad, I've reviewed financial statements *while* sitting in a lounge chair on a beach in Hawaii.

Maybe that's my "chop wood, carry water" sweet spot?

How about you? Where could work and enjoyment naturally intersect in your life? How could you change the scope of what you do to make it fun while expanding the value you create? Let me introduce you to some fantastic tools to start moving in that direction.

Unique Ability

I've referred to the entrepreneur coach Dan Sullivan a few times, and here's another nod to his teachings. Years ago, he and his wife published a book called *Unique Ability*, inspired by decades of working with high-performing professionals to help them find their optimal zone of performance. In the language of the above story, this process is about finding the activities that are both value-creating in a business sense while also being intrinsically fun and motivating for the individual doing them.

It's taken me years to zero in on my unique ability, a concept also taught by best-selling author Gay Hendricks in his book *Zone of Genius*. I've learned that we'll be making adjustments to our zone throughout life as we change and the world around us evolves. However, spending more time in this zone has become the goal of my "doing" each day. When I do, I'm at my best. Things flow and work can feel easy and fun.

Both of these books provide resources and a process to help readers discover their personal sweet spot. If you're serious about improving your relationship to work and moving to a bigger stage, I highly recommend you commit to doing this. Knowing your unique ability can feel like a superpower.

And a superpower is exactly what I needed as I looked to make this big pivot in my professional life. So my next step was to find out where my unique ability could be put to use in the business of acquiring income-producing assets.

To do this, I needed to identify the core activities of a full-time investor. What exactly does a person like that do all day?

Work the System

In my effort to get educated quickly on the finer points of multifamily acquisitions, I spent multiple weeks in 2022 deep in books, courses, and online forums. I listened to podcasts and found some big-time investors that had businesses that looked like what I desired to build. During one episode I recall vividly, the guest was the owner and leader of a large real estate investment management company, and he described the three primary functions of his firm as as (1) creating deal flow and underwriting assets, (2) raising capital and debt to fund the purchase, and (3) long-term asset management to execute the business plan.

Soon after, I took a course on deal analysis and capital raising. The instructor, a long-time multifamily investor, described his business using the exact same framework. This was reassuring, as it gave me confidence to understand what this business was going to look like long term.

With this framework in mind, I was able to identify the exact steps to take to build deal flow (a constant stream of new potential opportunities) and lay the foundation for raising capital (which would finance the acquisition of such opportunities). Specifically, I wrote down the following at the time:

1. Travel to and spend time in my target markets.
2. Earn the trust of the most influential brokers in town.
3. Underwrite a deal every day.
4. Issue letters of intent that make my stomach turn.
5. Build a list of bankers, attorneys, and property managers for each market.
6. Invite every professional I enjoy spending time with to a coffee meeting.
7. Hire a real estate and securities attorney.

I shared this list with multiple experienced investors and all agreed it was a straight path to a deal ... eventually. It was becoming clear that deal flow led to analysis. Analysis led to offers. Offers led to purchase and sale agreements (PSAs). PSAs led to closings. Closings led to ownership in deals and passive income.

It requires patience and focus and discipline, but history shows that new investors can uncover great opportunities due to their aggressive action and desire to get a deal to work.

This was the proven path. And I now offer it to you, so you too can see the road ahead as you move from novice to experience to professional real estate investor.

Moving ahead to the next chapter, I will introduce the concept of an investment thesis, a tool that clearly describes the exact assets you desire to acquire. The process of developing this thesis will require a focused effort, but luckily, I have a step-by-step system you can follow. All you need to do is work that system.

Chop wood. Carry water.

CHAPTER 9

Invest with Intent: Develop a Thesis

"Good afternoon, thanks for calling ABC Real Estate."

"Hi, I see this listing for a big apartment building in Des Moines. I'm an out-of-state investor and am interested in buying it."

"Okay, great, I can share all the financial information with you. But first, tell me a bit about yourself and how you invest."

"Awesome. I invest in real estate. Mainly apartments. Anywhere in the Midwest."

"Okay—what size deals are you after?"

"You know, anything with more than five doors."

"Got it. How about funding? How do you source funds to close your deals?"

"We raise the money from investors after getting a deal under contract."

"I see. Alright, what is your email?"

Although I'm withholding the identities of both parties to protect the innocent, this exchange occurred in early 2023 between a potential buyer and a multifamily broker that had recently listed a 48-unit property.

On the surface, the exchange is innocent enough. A simple back and forth between two people talking real estate shop. But to the veteran broker on one side of the phone—this was downright painful. They'd had some version of this call many times that month. Hundreds of times throughout their career. And they knew, with 99% certainty, that this buyer represented one thing: a waste of time.

I know this perspective because I had dinner with the broker shortly after this call came in. As we began our meal, he shared that time had taught him someone with such broad answers and lack of clear focus has a near zero chance of actually closing on a $5M asset.

He wants to see clarity in every topic he inquired with that buyer about and more. When a new out-of-state buyer calls into his niche market, he's excited. It means the market is expanding and getting national attention. But it also brings a lot of wantrepreneurs and newbies that are attempting to get into the apartment business but don't yet have the education, resources, and plan to be successful in that pursuit.

Let's not be one of those kinds of newbies. This chapter will ensure that doesn't happen by sharing my framework for developing a clear investment thesis and buy box for the assets you are going to pursue. I've learned that anything less results in a scattered strategy and sub-optimal purchases … or paralysis by analysis leading to no purchases at all.

Clarity and Conviction

The opposite of what this broker experienced on the phone is specificity. You know, like the sniper versus shotgun approach we learned from my special ops sales manager. Snipers have clarity on their target and don't pull the trigger until they have conviction. And that conviction is developed by being specific. When I say specific, I mean *specific*.

"Apartment buildings in the Midwest" is neither a buy box nor a strategy. That is a general category that contains hundreds of sizes, types, conditions, and strategies within it.

Contrast that with something like "50 to 150 units, garden-style multifamily communities built after 1980, located in the Des Moines metropolitan statistical area (MSA) with in-place monthly rents exceeding 1% of unit purchase price and room to grow long-term yield-on-cost 200 basis points above entry."

With a statement like this, the broker assumes they are dealing with a real deal investor. Any broker covering Des Moines can hear that and immediately narrow down a niche group of assets and owners in their mind to fit the description. Constraints such as these can reduce a market of thousands of properties down to a couple hundred. And of that few hundred, maybe five or ten of them will trade, or even consider to be traded in a given year.

This is specificity. *This* is a business plan. And *this* enables this broker, and the bankers, insurance agents, property managers, general contractors, and eventually a few hundred residents that you will need to work with to know what you're doing and that you have a path to success.

The stated buy box above also happens to be exactly what Greg and I look for in one of our target markets. Importantly, it didn't always look like this. We developed it over time as we learned and played the game. And it will continue to evolve. In five years, I can guarantee it will be different. We'll likely still be going after apartments in Des Moines, but the criteria will change.

Sophisticated Opinions

Let's back up a bit and lay some foundation for our topic. An investment thesis is a reasoned argument for a particular investment strategy, backed up by research and analysis. It's a documented set of beliefs and boundaries, a framework that drives the decisions of an investor.

Coming into this business, it was obvious that I needed some clarity around just what I would be investing in. I expect this will be true for you as well. There are a lot of decisions to make before an aspiring investor can even start to "look" for potential investments to qualify. But it wasn't until my first few meetings with some local family offices that were considering investing with me that I realized how the truly sophisticated investors worked. They had strong opinions about certain markets, assets, and strategies. They had boundaries and limits. They had specific underwriting standards, legal requirements, and mandatory tax structures. They had considered everything.

What stood out even more was the level of conviction these individuals held in their thesis. Among the best of these investors, there was absolutely no violating of current

boundaries. If some aspect of a deal falls outside their constraints—then they don't do it. As showcased in Chapter 7,
having clear constraints and the discipline to respect those
constraints is a very powerful combination. These investors
created that boundary for a reason. At the same time, all of
these investment veterans were open to discussing the finer
points of their thesis and were up for friendly debate. Many
were interested in hearing counterpoints and reviewing data
sources which conflicted with their own. They didn't claim to
be right, but rather, clear in their opinion and beliefs.

Another point I picked up in these meetings: a good thesis is
the result of a strong narrative on economic and demographic
trends. Savvy investors don't start buying industrial buildings
because they heard the industrial sector is hot right now.
No, they start buying industrial buildings because their
research indicates that e-commerce delivery will replace
retail shopping over the next 40 years and big companies like
Amazon will have a near endless need for last-mile delivery
facilities. Further, the investor believes in the population
trends of two specific cities and finds that the total supply
of industrial space in development is still short of demand
forecasts. All of this turns into an investment thesis around
industrial buildings of a certain size with loading bays and
good access to highways across a dozen zip codes.

That sounds like a high probability strategy and it shows how
the experts use their thesis to play this game at a high level.
Investors who don't carry a strong thesis will watch all the
industrial buildings go up in their area and decide to get in
on these assets after they hear about industrial sector growth
in the news. By then, the first investor is cashing out on
their projects and are ready to buy land that will eventually

be used to build AI datacenters. You get the point—a thesis gives direction and will allow you to see opportunities that are not obvious to the general public.

A final note before we move to the process of developing your own opinion—there is no such thing as a correct answer. Stating the obvious—unique investors have unique goals, timelines, and risk tolerances. Those differences require unique assets and strategies to accomplish.

Here's a great example of how different opinions can be, yet both be completely correct for that individual investor. I met with one local family that wouldn't buy anything built before 1990. They don't like the maintenance risk. The next week, I sat down with a small private equity fund that wouldn't buy anything built after 1990. They demand a level of cash flow from their assets that couldn't be achieved in newer buildings. A great thesis isn't one that accurately predicts the future, although we certainly make some attempts to that end. Instead, a great thesis is one that is based in reason, is backed by data, and inspires confidence in the investor to move forward with acquiring assets to fit.

So how do you go about coming up with such a clearly defined target?

Developing a Thesis

Here is the simple five-step method I used to develop my own opinion and create a clear investing thesis to drive my business forward and I suggest you employ as well.

1. State Investment Goals

Like the classic advice states, you need to know where you're going in order to get there. The first step of any professional undertaking should likely be to set some goals and form a definition of success. Statements like "making money" or "earning a good return" are not valid investing goals. These are not inspiring, and they have no boundaries.

Instead, I believe we can be incredibly clear on what we are going for: the Four Freedoms. I aim for those freedoms so I can be the best dad and husband possible to my family. This desire brings with it some clear financial goals, like replacing my prior earned income with cash flow from apartment investing. I also had specific steps along the way—like buying a 100-unit building and then building a portfolio of similar buildings.

I work with a number of investors that take the role of limited partner (LP) in our projects. We'll discuss more about that function in Chapter 16. Although many of these investors' goals look the same on the surface, I've learned to dig and uncover the deeper drivers and reasons why they're investing. Some of them do it for cash flow like me. Some of them have huge income from other sources, so they invest almost purely for tax efficiency. Many others do it for some form of legacy—to leave for their children, to pay for their grandchildren's education, or to increase resources before they put those resources to work in philanthropic efforts.

All of these are acceptable investment goals. The most important part is that they are intrinsically motivating and written down, so they can drive the next step in the process.

2. Perform Market Research

Once we have clarity on our initial goals and we've documented them—I also shared mine with mentors and coaches—it's time to start digging into the data. Most importantly, we need to find a few markets to focus on. For commercial real estate that means understanding a number of key statistics:

- Population and demographic trends
- Employment and income trends
- Political and legal trends

As a few potential markets that met all my initial criteria began to stack up, I could then move more granular to understand how real estate was playing out in each of these locations. Although investor sentiment and credit markets often move together on a national level, real estate is highly localized. Different cities can experience unique cycles that might be out of sync with the broader picture. So after isolating a metropolitan statistical area (MSA), I recommend looking to uncover what is happening in the following areas:

- Local property values and housing supply
- Local economic drivers and threats
- Local insurance standards and lending terms
- Local politics and advocacy trends
- Local construction and development pipeline

Of course, there are plenty of other topics to consider. Crime ratings, tax assessments, and local nuances in real estate and renting laws are important as well. Eventually, you'll start flying to the target cities and communicating with local experts who have context and knowledge down to the street level.

To get the process started, we can leverage that amazing thing called the internet and its endless resources to find critical data. To save you some time, I'm sharing the sites I found to be most useful and that I still refer back to regularly as I update my market research:

- *Texas Real Estate Research Center* (trerc.tamu.edu): This site, hosted by Texas A&M University, might seem like an odd choice as my single favorite site to look up real estate data, but the school has invested into great online tools to quickly access and visualize the key metrics of population and employment around the country. You can sort by state or by MSA and compare data since they began collecting it. Most areas have 50-plus years of annual data on the most important metrics. The site also allows downloading of the data into spreadsheets, so you can slice and dice further if so inclined.
- *LoopNet* (loopnet.com): This website is the closest thing to Zillow for commercial properties. The first thing to understand—most good deals never see the light of LoopNet. High-volume brokers don't use LoopNet, institutions don't buy from LoopNet, and it has never played a role in any of my acquisitions. However, the site is still an aggregator of property information, and there are stories of investors winning great deals that were listed here. Early on, I spent a lot of time on the site simply because it has tons of data. There are offering memos and financial statements for properties around the nation. These

provided early examples to practice my underwriting and deal analysis. On this site I even met a few brokers that I still talk to today.

The data upon which Texas A&M and thousands of other sites sort and display are provided by the two federal agencies below. One focuses on counting people and the other on counting jobs. I find these sites cumbersome to navigate although sometimes worth it to gather a specific data point:

- *US Census Bureau* (census.gov): Every ten years, the US government goes on the official mission of counting every person living in the country. In the process, they've created 2.5 million tables of raw data, maps, profiles, and other demographic information. All of it can be accessed at no charge on their website.

- *US Bureau of Labor Statistics* (bls.gov): The stock market and financial industry obsesses over periodic reports like the consumer price index and the employment situation, each published monthly. The BLS is responsible for these and thousands of other reports regarding the employment of US citizens, their income, and purchasing power. This site enables free access to all of these reports.

Another source of official data from a federal institution that has great influence over credit markets and property values is the following:

- *FRED* (fred.stlouisfed.org): An acronym for Federal Reserve Economic Data, FRED is a very popular tool for macroeconomic charts and graphs. Metrics around GDP, the money supply, inflation, and similar measures are published on this site. It's free of charge and produces powerful charts that can be customized and filtered live on your screen.

A final group of resources, the two sites below are paid platforms. It's not necessary to have either of these to be successful at commercial real estate. However, as I got more involved in the market and started issuing letters of intent (LOIs) in excess of $10M, spending money on tools to access better market data started to make more sense.

- *Crexi Intelligence* (crexi.com): An aggregator of property and transaction information, this is an entry-level paid tool for market intelligence. Its interface and tools are designed to work just like Zillow, so the navigation is simple, but this site is exclusive to commercial properties. Its data is good but often incomplete. It provides sales history on most assets, maps with crime and demographic overlays, and even details on debt maturities for some properties. This would be my recommended first step into paying for data tools.
- *CoStar* (costar.com): An industry leader, CoStar plays a dominant role in the collection and dissemination of data regarding the sales and operations of commercial real estate. Just about every major real estate business, once they get to a certain size, bites the bullet to get access to this tool. It's prohibitively expensive, and licensing is highly protected. However, it also enables you to type an address and moments later get a 150-page report detailing every market fundamental you could think of. Maybe you get what you pay for?

3. Define Criteria and Constraints

This step is where you continue to define and refine, getting more and more specific. Let me explain. As I was digging through the mountains of data available and trying to make sense of it all, I reminded myself that the whole goal of that research period was to create constraints. As mentioned before, this whole business of having an opinion is a process that takes time. While putting in my time, I would discover an important data point or trend and document it so as to keep alive the markets and strategies that fit. Then I would find another data point that represented risks or challenges that I wasn't interested in, and I would document those and turn it into a new boundary. Day by day, my playing field was getting more clearly defined.

I'll emphasize here that this step is all about reduction and elimination. Each new item you add to this list will appropriately reduce your options, rejecting everything that isn't a fit. This can be a challenge, and you'll likely feel resistance to this. Refer to Chapter 7 for a refresher on why constraints are good.

4. Develop a Game Plan

Once the framework of your beliefs and opinions about the market is documented, it's time to move to developing your conviction and outlining your action plan. I had done much of this work while spending months getting educated on the business. Most of the coaches and programs I pulled from provided a list of key activities, and there wasn't much variance between the lists.

Everyone agreed that in order to win a deal, you must be spending time in the target market, getting face time with brokers, underwriting every deal, submitting LOIs, and getting approved with banks and lenders. I've also seen that creating relationships with the most influential property managers, insurance brokers, city officials, general contractors, and real estate attorneys in a given market will serve you very well long term.

Another important piece of this step is creating some kind of timeline. I've been taught by my experience in business and investing that patience is a requirement for success. You simply can't force a result to occur by a certain time. With that said, it's useful to put some target on the board. High achievers often stress themselves out by setting arbitrary deadlines and then defining their internal worth via their attainment of that goal. Accordingly, I include timelines to keep myself motivated but try to not beat myself up because something took longer to happen than I desired.

This action of creating a plan has the wonderful side effect of generating confidence and conviction within you. By mentally practicing how you could deal with the obstacles that are sure to rise, you fortify yourself against those challenges and you'll be far more likely to continue on and see it through.

5. Implement and Iterate

The opposite mistake of not having a thesis or opinion is to develop one and then lock into it so tight that it never changes. Far from a one-time decision, the approach I recommend is about maintaining a thesis and updating it as the environment around you changes. There are times where you'll learn new information that you never considered before, and you'll go back to the drawing board to see how it affects your holistic view. One data point should not swing the whole stack, but it could open you up to new directions long term.

This process is highly iterative. Starting at step one, you audit your situation and goals. Then you perform more research and clarify your constraints. You use those constraints to build a plan and get to work executing that plan. Your work will provide feedback, which you can use to better inform the answers to step one, and you start again.

Law of the First Deal

While working the process above, the first opportunity to apply my developing thesis presented itself rather quickly. It was April 2022, fewer than 90 days into my "let's do apartments" journey—and I received an excited phone call from Greg. He had been contacted by a peer and local investor regarding a 16-unit property that he had under contract.

The apartment was located about an hour away from us and had a very compelling story. It was situated on a busy street near the University of California Riverside's campus and was fully occupied, but had an absentee owner who had let maintenance and tenant quality fall over the years.

Additionally, the investor that was acquiring it had a straight-forward business plan that made practical sense. He was going to bring a big capital budget to the deal and fix all outstanding maintenance issues and renovate every unit to a modern standard. By doing so, he projected he could increase rents by 20% to 30%, which would increase the asset's value considerably and provide a healthy return.

There was just one problem—he was short on the cash needed to make that business plan come together and, therefore, open to partnering with us if we could help close the gap. After a few meetings and some deep analysis and due diligence on our side, I made the decision that this would be a perfect deal to start and engage the Law of the First Deal.

The next four weeks were trial by fire. I learned so darn much helping to put that deal together, it's hard to give it proper credit. But we closed on time, and I earned a material stake in the deal as a co-manager.

With the wisdom of hindsight—I can share that two years later, this project has primarily served to inform me of new constraints I place on future deals. There are aspects of this asset that have created challenges: the small door count, the level of repairs needed, the short-term mortgage, the low cap rates, and challenging landlord restrictions in California.

Importantly, these nuances are really tough to learn from the sidelines because none of these attributes make this an objectively bad deal. On the contrary, I know investors who have become filthy rich mastering those exact points. These investors accept more volatility and headaches than I'm willing to, but that doesn't make 100-unit deals in Iowa better than 17-unit deals in Riverside. Rather, it simply informs that one is a better fit for me and my goals.

That is what the Law of the First deal can do for you. It's the practical action of Step 5 in my process above by providing feedback on your initial thesis to help it mature and improve.

Sticking with It

I'll close this topic out with the wisdom of a world heavy-weight boxing champion. Mike Tyson once famously said:

Everyone has a plan until they get punched in the mouth.

And yes—sometimes investing can feel like getting punched in the mouth. It is never a straight path. There will be twists and turns and moments of doubt. In the short term, the value of assets can swing up and down while new risks to the investment will come and go. If the investment is a stock or operating company, executives will fail and get fired. If it's a rental property, there will be evictions and surprise capital expenses. It's all part of the game.

The true winners of the investment game continue to be those who can stick to their plan. I've seen examples of investors being wildly successful with all sorts of strategies and asset classes. They don't have to invest in risky markets or risky assets. They also don't always follow conventional strategies. As stated in previous chapters—it all can work.

But one thing successful investors (those who stick around a long time and gain the Four Freedoms) all have in common— they stay convicted to their beliefs and plans. They don't buy things that fall outside their zone. And they don't freak out and sell something just because it is running into some challenges.

In fact, the trigger-happy investor is always the biggest loser— the one that doesn't stick to a plan and moves from strategy to strategy, looking for quick wins—this does not work. It never has. The financial industry has proven this over and over with decades of data. The only way to win in this game is to play it long term and stay committed to a thesis that makes practical sense given the environment around you.

If you think your investment thesis will hold up, stick with it through thick and thin. Resilience during tough times is one of the primary reasons to have a thesis. It's your source of truth within all the noise of markets.

Next up, we'll start to apply this thesis to potential investments by focusing on an often overlooked strategy—scale.

CHAPTER 10

Doors, Doors, Doors: Strategies to Scale

This book started with a story about my business partner Greg explaining a real estate investment strategy that focused on scale. His rationale for this direction was all about reducing risk. "With three units, one empty unit is a 33% loss of revenue. With 100 units, one empty unit is a 1% loss of revenue." As we would learn diving deep into the world of buying and owning these assets, there is a lot more benefit to scaling than reducing vacancy risk. In fact, that's just the start.

After "getting my feet wet" on the first deal by partnering on the Riverside project, I was officially a multifamily investor and ready to start the search for the next deal. I can remember there being a single focus in my mind—finding a 100-unit apartment worthy of buying.

One day in June, we were contacted by another investor, Mike, who we had met a few weeks prior through a referral. The first deal we talked about with him didn't work out, but we stayed in touch and were pleased when he reached out about a new opportunity. This time, he had a property in

Waco, Texas under contract. Mike shared his team's initial underwriting as well as the supporting documents like the property's rent roll and financial statements.

After a quick review of the numbers, he had our full attention. The rent and expense assumptions that they were using to underwrite the purchase were highly conservative. At a time when everyone in the market was underwriting frothy assumptions with the idea that debt would be cheap forever, I was amazed at how reasonable their expectations were.

Greg and I continued our research and discovered this really was a "deal." Compared to recent sales, the cost basis was well under market. They had an agreement at a $9.9M purchase price, but an argument could easily have been made for a $12M valuation. Finally, the location of the property was simply amazing. The community sat on the border of Baylor University, and much of its rent roll was composed of students, faculty, and staff at the school.

And the cherry on top—it had 96 units … darn close to 100!

As fate would have it, Greg and I were set to fly to Dallas for a conference right as we were getting wind of this deal. We would be within a 90-minute drive of the property. I was beginning to develop a strong hunch this property was going to be our "100 unit" vision realized, so I canceled my return flight after the conference and stayed a couple of extra days to drive down to Waco and spend time at and around the property. Meanwhile, Greg flew back and focused on all the data and reports we had available to complete our due diligence list.

Everything checked out for Greg, and my visit to Waco was nothing short of inspiring. The buildings were in great shape and had a charm I had not expected for a property with this kind of upside potential. We loved the deal and committed to joining forces with Mike and his team. This time Greg and I signed up to bring $2M of investor equity to the party, in addition to asset management responsibilities.

This was a big commitment, but we had confidence we could pull it off. I had continued my Coffee Campaign with new energy after the Riverside deal closed. That effort resulted in a long list of individuals and families that expressed interest in the deals I was talking about.

When the time came, I reached out to these high-potential contacts to advise them of the opportunity. To efficiently share my enthusiasm, I recorded a five-minute video where I outlined my "Top Five Deal Points" and described why I was investing my own money in the deal.

The next few days brought a lot of phone calls. I racked up hundreds of dials and hours of talk time as I walked a number of high-trust relationships through the finer points of the deal. Just 72 hours after sending out the video, all $2M of capital was spoken for by 17 unique investors. I was overwhelmed with gratitude and also realized just how much demand there was from individual investors for high-quality real estate backed by a high-quality thesis.

And clearly, the Law of the First Deal was in full effect because this deal was, indeed, easier—despite being multiple times larger and a thousand miles away.

An Abundance of Advantages

This story illustrates many of the lessons learned thus far about vision, focus, constraints, and doing the work. Now let's explore the power of scale in the business of income-producing assets and how you can put this advantage to work in your investment strategy. Adding to the lessons of risk mitigation from the previous chapter, we now build on that and highlight a long list of benefits we have witnessed and experienced from the scale provided by hundreds of dwellings under one parcel.

Favorable Lending

The first thing I noticed when making the switch from single-family rentals to multifamily assets is how different the lending terms were. I have a graduate degree in accounting and finance, and I've taken out more loans than I can remember in my day. But the first commercial loan quotes that came back had terms and conditions I had never seen before:

- DSCR, LTV, and LTC
- I/O period and interest reserves
- Yield maintenance and defeasance

Those last two took months for me to fully understand but have massive implications for the ability to exit a loan after it's issued. We will actually define all of these terms and more in the next chapter on leverage (and in the Appendix), but for now, let's just recognize that commercial real estate loans have a lot more ways to be customized to improve their value to the borrower and reduce their risk to the lender.

Today, I absolutely love the complexity and flexibility of commercial debt. It allows for the right loan to match the right project. Some deals need high leverage for short periods, so the investor can complete big repairs and then get refinanced out afterwards. Other acquisitions require less leverage, but investors look for long periods (ten-plus years) of fixed and known debt cost. There is a loan product available for each of these and just about every other situation that comes up.

The other observation I had on those first debt quotes could be summarized in a simple rule that continues to hold true: the bigger the balance, the better the terms. In fact, the rates on large apartment loans are the lowest that can be secured for any investment asset. This is because of the statistic I shared earlier about the percentage of multifamily borrowers that experience extended delinquency or default. It's extremely low, under 1% historically, so the "risk premium" on multifamily loans is low.

The reason for this "bigger is better" regarding debt makes sense: issuing a loan is a very labor-intensive process. For the lender, there are so many boxes to check and risks to mitigate. Those boxes and risks are the same, whether it's a $1M or $100M loan. Once the loan is booked, 95% of the work is done and most go on autopilot for years. The more cash you take out, the more efficiency the bank gains, and the less each borrowed dollar costs in origination overhead.

Budget for Staff

My years as an entrepreneur in the technology industry provided me with a great appreciation for staff and building a business as a team. We had zero employees for the first nine months of my company. That meant I packed every box and printed every FedEx label until we brought on that first help in the warehouse. It would be months more until we produced enough revenue to support hiring an assistant to help with operations and customer communication.

On the contrary, in the business of commercial multifamily assets, the buildings an investor acquires are usually full of residents paying rent. That recurring revenue comes with the building and provides the investor a budget from day one to hire staff that can execute the day-to-day operations of the property.

As a general rule, expect a full-time leasing agent and full-time maintenance staff to manage every 100 doors. These numbers vary widely based on different operators and the class of property, but in today's market, this rule works out to around $1,200 per door annually. So our 96 units in Waco example would equate to $115,200 in budget for staff.

Although staffing property management positions can be a challenge even with a budget, this built-in assumption that staff will be needed to operate the building was welcome. When I was considering the triplex in Costa Mesa, I was thinking about managing it myself. Is that cost-efficient? Yes. Is it thinking small and putting my future freedoms at risk? Yeah, that too.

Less Management, More Leadership

Generally speaking, the smaller and more local an investment property is, the more hands on it will be for the owner. This is due to the fact that small properties don't generate enough income to pay for staff or others to do the work, and the proximity usually turns into frequent visits.

The flip side of this is true as well—the larger the asset, the more likely it will be managed by an external team that is then led by the owner. Properties with hundreds of units have more inbound calls, leasing tours, maintenance requests, and administrative duties than one person could handle in the first place. And as the size increases, so does the overall budget, allowing for the hiring of specialists and even layers of reporting and decision-making before it gets to the owner.

I once heard this dynamic referred to as "boardroom executive versus job-site foreman." I think that actually is a decent visualization. And for me, I'm a boardroom kind of guy. I spent 20 years of my career trying to get into other companies' boardrooms to talk shop and potentially earn a new customer. Greg had a similar experience with 15 years of discovery and presentations to executives in their boardrooms. Reading through high-level reports and making decisions based on the information was my favorite part of running a business. Having a team to work with and lead is a "get-to" for me; whereas I can't claim to be a handyman and would waste a lot of time and money learning how to do basic home repairs.

This industry is full of property management firms that specialize in the execution of rental property operations. Much like issuing a loan, processing a lease involves a ton of paperwork and checking of boxes. It would be totally overwhelming to try to create all the forms, organize the information, and comply with every applicable law. From my perspective, property management is a function that can be successfully outsourced to another company that does it at scale.

I'm in a much better position to grow and achieve those Four Freedoms when I'm working on a business, or leading, than when I'm working in a business, or managing.

Systems and Best Practices

An underappreciated aspect of scale to most, "systems" might be my favorite as it relates to the freedoms I'm going after. I spent many years suffering at the mercy of an inbox and internal need to respond quickly to every little thing. It wasn't until some great business coaches got involved in my life and challenged me to figure out systems to outsource the repetitive work that it all changed for me.

You know what kind of work is hard to create systems for? Nuanced, customized, and creative work.

You know what kind of work is easy to create systems around? Routine tasks that repeat on a regular basis.

Now think about what needs to happen at a well-run apartment: collect rent on the first of each month, approve maintenance requests each morning, give leasing tours each afternoon, process applications as they come through. It's all very routine work that happens on a regular schedule.

Accordingly, I have been a kid in a candy store watching these businesses work. We have partnered with some awesome property managers who handle 99% of the operational burden of the assets we control. And anytime a decision does reach us at the ownership level, if at all possible, I put it into a category and create some type of rule for future occurrences.

With one property, this approach is silly. Everything is a one-off situation when you have one door. But with hundreds of doors, systems are essential and create a better experience for the owners, staff, and residents.

Expense Efficiencies

Simply put, when you buy more stuff, you have more leverage to get better terms. However, it's not as easy as "squeezing a vendor" and demanding a lower price. In fact, I've witnessed a number of methods to extract short-term concessions that end up back-firing over the long-term.

On the other hand, there are highly strategic ways to align with vendors to help them get what they want and, in the process, receive the absolute best pricing and terms in the industry. A good example would be for an item like flooring. Rather than simply calling a local warehouse and asking for a discount, you could ask what flooring products they are overstocked on; then offer to clean out those slow-moving products for a heavy discount. We did this exact move on a project in Des Moines and got enough flooring for 40 units at the price of 20 units. These types of win-win situations are how you can gain long-term cost advantages with vendors that like you and want to see you succeed.

Longer Hold Periods

In the world of commercial real estate, the period of time from acceptance of an offer to the actual closing of the transaction is typically 60 days. There are situations where it's shorter, and there are plenty of situations where it goes longer. Transacting on these assets also costs a few percentage points of the price in commissions and fees, which can easily be hundreds of thousands of dollars. In other words, these are fairly illiquid assets, meaning they are hard to turn into cash.

Compare this to a stock on the NASDAQ. I have an online broker, so turning that stock into cash takes about one second and has nearly zero transaction fees. That is a highly liquid asset. It's company stock one moment, and it's cash the next. (Stocks are also a highly volatile asset class that makes them a poor strategic choice for liquid holdings, but that's a lesson for another day.)

This concept of liquidity, like most investing levers, cuts both ways. On the surface, the inability to quickly turn an apartment into cash is seen as a drawback or negative feature. But experience has taught me the opposite—it's actually one of the asset class's best traits. Because real estate is expensive and time-consuming to sell, people think twice before selling. Which means they hold on to the assets much longer than they hold other things, like stocks. As an owner, I've seen this effect basically "force" me to hold longer than my short-term emotions would prefer.

If those rental homes in Jacksonville could have been sold like stock, I likely would have cut them years before I did. Every single one of them had an "oh crap" moment where

I was dumping money into them to cure unforeseen issues. Trigger-happy investors sell assets that do this. But because of their illiquidity, I did the repairs and held on for years after. And every single one of them turned around and outperformed my expectations over the long term.

Compounding Returns

The idea of compounding is one of those things that's totally boring in the beginning and totally mind-blowing once it has enough time to work. I originally understood its power from the "doubling a penny" example.

> *If you double a penny every day for a week, you get 64 cents. If you double a penny every day for a month, you get ... $5,368,709.12.*

Crazy but true. Let's take the most famous investor of all time, Warren Buffett, to showcase this via example. In the book, *Psychology of Money*, the author Morgan Housel shares a story about the key to Buffett's success and the building of his legendary portfolio. The truth is that most of the money that he has today, his billions of dollars, were not made till after his 70th birthday. In fact, if he had started investing at 25 years old like a normal person and stopped at retirement age like a normal person, his net worth would be $12 million, not $90 billion. He's literally a thousand times wealthier because he stayed with it for two extra decades. Key takeaway—hold periods matter.

Meanwhile, the investing world continues to search for the answers to Buffet's success. It must be his analysis? Or his risk-taking? Or his deal-making? Well, the data says 99% of his net worth can be tied to little more than the amount of time he has been investing. That's how compounding works. It is incredibly powerful, but it is not intuitive. I've done the math on that doubling penny more than once because it just doesn't seem to make sense.

A big takeaway here is the reminder that when it comes to real estate, we need to think like Buffett with a timeframe of decades, not as an options trader or crypto bro who thinks in days or weeks. The first gets huge tailwinds to their results via the compounding effect; and it gets better every year. For the latter, there is no compounding, and every day starts at zero.

Scale Leads to More Scale

A final point on the power of scale—it can become a virtuous cycle. As you add properties and doors, you gain efficiencies and improve your systems. You also clarify your thesis and build out your team. These improvements provide you an advantage in the local market, and you rightfully improve your odds of winning other deals that trade in the area. Those additional properties would lead to even more efficiencies in your team, knowledge in the market, and economies of scale. And on it goes ...

Of course, scale is not a panacea. It does not fix all problems, and there is a point of getting too big. Or better said, too big for the operator and their level of skill, systems, and resources.

Scaling, and the speed of scale, will be highly dependent on a number of factors unique to each investor. To help you land in the right place, let's talk about how to scale the right way.

Strategies to Scale

It's one thing to agree with the points above; it's another to implement them into your investing future. Here are some key points I've learned the hard way as I worked towards putting scale as a core part of my strategy. The markets you choose, the people you work with, the method of raising equity—all of it needs to be purposeful to get the benefits of scale.

Capital and Debt

Nothing will restrict the scale of an investment portfolio like the availability of cash to buy assets. If the plan is to go big, then the sources of capital need to be plentiful. There is no right way to do this—some people earn it at a day job, some people inherit it, most people need to raise it from their peers and network; but to buy quality assets with good risk-adjusted returns, you need millions of dollars in cash. The type of people that you invest with will dictate the scale.

The same goes for sources of debt. There are only a handful of direct lenders that can give investors access to "agency" mortgages, something we'll cover in the next chapter. These are by far the most accretive loans on the market, yet many young investors with big dreams don't have relationships with a direct lender or the confidence to approach one. They hide behind local brokers they feel comfortable with but who can't offer the terms available when dealing directly with Fannie Mae or Freddie Mac.

Qualifying for debt is another consideration. As a limited partner (LP), this is not a concern. You can invest in thousands of doors and never be on the loan. But as a sponsor or general partner (GP), there has to be a member of the team applying for the loan with deep pockets of documented assets (Chapters 15 and 16 discuss LPs and GPs). My story in the next chapter shares how essential this was early on in Greg and my growth and success with scaling.

Markets and Inventory

This is a point I did not consider until I attempted to build deal flow in multiple markets simultaneously. By doing so, it became clear how some MSAs are loaded with large apartment communities that trade frequently. It became equally obvious that other cities simply don't have a lot of inventory, and you can go crazy trying to dig up deals where there are none.

Obviously, the volume of inventory will have a correlation to the population of that market, but not all zip codes are created equally. Due to zoning restrictions and home owners lobbying for low-density housing to surround their homes, some markets have very few large apartment communities. Using the tools shared in the last chapter, you can get a great sense for the total door and asset count in an area. Additionally, all the national brokers publish their annual deal volume by MSA.

I've considered this and know exactly how much of my target market's total inventory I would need to buy to hit our goals. The truth is, a single market would not be enough for what Greg and I are trying to accomplish—hence why we have two core markets with a total of nearly a thousand properties we'd love to own at the right time and right price.

I'd encourage you to spend the time necessary to understand the inventory and deal volumes for any asset class and location you're considering. It can save you years of frustration later.

Team and Partners

The points above drive home the idea that it matters who you are working with. There are tons of great property managers (PMs), but not all of them are great for a 180-unit deal with on-site amenities. If that's the kind of asset you are targeting, then make sure you know the best PM for that kind of asset. I've learned there are probably only four or five companies in any market that can really deliver great results for third-party owners.

The term "joint venture" (JV) is one that I'd encourage you to get comfortable with. It refers to a business arrangement where two or more parties agree to pool their resources for the purposes of achieving specific goals. It also implies sharing risks and responsibilities, but importantly—defines those very clearly in a legal agreement. I have used JVs as a fast path to nearly 1,000 units in two years.

By focusing on what we are great at and finding a like-minded partner that was great at other aspects and valued our contribution—Greg and I, as well as our partner, have been able to buy stuff that none of us could have done alone. Even better, it eliminates competition! Rather than always bidding against other talented investors, you can be on the same team. As the book continues, I'll share stories of some opportunistic purchases that were only possible due to a joint venture approach. The two parties have a mutual interest in the success of projects, and this has kept us all accountable through the term of the projects.

Scale as Way to Manage Risk

At the end of the day, I keep coming back to scale and its ability to reduce volatility and risk. Let's look back at my original intent that, I'd expect, is yours as well—to find an investment asset and career that played on a big scale yet had a high probability of success. I chose commercial multifamily real estate and have been validated in that direction thus far, despite the macro headwinds facing the industry.

No doubt, a decision to bring scale as part of the core strategy also means a decision to delay gratification and play a longer game. Bigger assets often take longer to stabilize, but like a cast iron skillet, they hold the heat much better over the long term.

When applied correctly, scale can help you reduce risk and improve returns. Now it's time to move on to discussing the best practices on how you can finance a property and apply the proper use of leverage.

CHAPTER 11

Leveraging Your Biggest Investor

It started with a small sketch on a scrap piece of paper. In fact, a lot of big, life-changing ideas start like that.

Southwest Airlines was famously started on a cocktail napkin when a pilot and a lawyer were having drinks at a bar in San Antonio, Texas. The pilot, Rollin King, drew a triangle, with the words Dallas, Houston, and San Antonio at each corner of the triangle. Frustrated with the high cost of air travel and lack of options for travelers at that time (1966), he described an airline that would focus on intrastate travel and by doing so, create efficiency and be able to offer low-cost seats like the market had never seen before.

The lawyer, Herb Kelleher, saw the value proposition and market need but also understood the mountain of challenges that would lay in front of anyone starting an airline. Purchasing a fleet of airplanes and fighting competitive and regulatory battles was going to be a very expensive endeavor. That part was obvious to him as soon as the triangle was drawn.

"Where," Kelleher asked King, "would we get the capital?"

To which King responded, "Capital? Oh, I guess we'll have to raise it."

As the story goes, upon hearing this, Kelleher lowered his head for a moment to rub his eyes, then looked up, and said: "Rollin, you're crazy. Let's do it."

We start this chapter with an anecdote about big things that come from small beginnings and require a ton of resources to make happen. Like Herb Kelleher, one big question that is likely circling through your head right now is: "'Where would I get the capital' to partake in all this income-producing asset business?"

With that, I'd like to share a story of how the next big deal came together for me. It contains some amazing lessons on how to "find the capital" and leverage your biggest investor— who might not be who you currently think it's going to be.

The Napkin Plan

Back on my personal journey, let's move ahead to July 2022. The Waco project had closed, so Greg and I had some celebrating to do. We needed to take a moment to appreciate what had just happened. Namely the $2M of outside investor capital that came our way and the great property that we now had a significant ownership stake in.

Additionally, there were some big life and work changes to recognize. Greg had officially exited his executive role and the partnership status at his consulting firm. We now had a taste of what big real estate deals looked like, and it was clear that this can and would become a full-time job if we wanted to go big. Accordingly, we had formalized our partnership and created Measured Capital LLC to hold all of our general partnership shares (that's the sweat equity that sponsors gain for putting together and managing deals).

On a Friday afternoon, we met at a restaurant and spent a few hours discussing what we had accomplished to that point and also to talk about where we wanted to go. Much like King and Kelleher above, we were thinking big, and we were talking crazy. No constraints for this conversation; it was all about "what's possible."

Rather than a napkin, I broke out a pad of paper, and at the very top of the sheet, I wrote the word "Measured." Over the next hour, an inspired conversation compelled me to write the following list, our "napkin plan":

1. Markets: Des Moines (100+ units), Jacksonville (80+), SoCal (40+)
2. Criteria: 1970–80s, garden style, C+ or B-,
3. Equity raise: $5M raise = $15M purchase price
4. Key principals: Mike, Jeff, Gary, Aaron, David …
5. Next deal: lead sponsor, under contract by August

I'll admit a triangle with three words is a far more elegant way to sketch a business plan, but these five bullet points and the ideas they contain ended up being very effective for us. We both took a picture of this sheet and referred back to it constantly as we worked to make it come true during the following months.

We didn't waste any time getting to work. Within a week of this meeting, Greg and I were on a plane heading for Des Moines, Iowa and a four-day trip to explore this market and its potential. Of course, we had been talking to the brokers and analyzing deals there well before this trip. But I also knew from my experience of the Coffee Campaign that face-to-face meetings had the value of potentially hundreds of phone and email interactions.

The Jefferson

So we packed our schedule and sat down with every influential person in Des Moines real estate that would take a meeting with us. On that first visit, we learned of a deal called The Jefferson, a 108-unit community just a few miles south of downtown. Our initial take was that it was too expensive, and we didn't give it much attention.

But on a follow-up visit a month later, Greg toured the property and met with the on-site management team, including one member of the group that owned it. This time, he got the sense that there was opportunity, and we decided to analyze the deal in depth. The broker handling the deal provided us with the historical financial statements as well as the current rent roll.

We decided, after thorough analysis, that we'd love to purchase it if we could get the price to $8M, a big reduction from its asking price of $9M. We wrote up an offer and submitted it to the broker, but did one thing to stand out. I recorded a video of myself and presented our rationale, intent, and background. This little tweak turned out to open some doors we never really could have imagined.

That's because I made sure to explain our debt assumptions to the seller. The increased cost of the mortgage payments is what was driving our demand for a lower price. This resulted in the broker calling us back and informing us that there was a great loan already financing the property. Maybe we could convince the local bank in Iowa to transfer the current mortgage as is. (This is a process known as "loan assumption.")

Some brief background here—the Jefferson had been purchased 18 months prior by a company named VareCo and a principal investor named Terrance. When they acquired it, they secured a $4.7M loan at 3.5% interest rate. For reference, mortgage rates were quickly moving into the 6% range as we got serious about buying it.

Let's stop for a second to make sure we recognize the impact of this. At 3.5% rate, the annual interest cost is $164,500 each year. A mortgage on the same balance and 6% interest rate comes to $282,000 per year. That's nearly $120k difference. Every year!

To take the calculation a step further, let's look at net cash flow in each situation. At the time, the property was generating $320,000 in annual operating income. So that means the net cash flows (the stuff you actually keep) is $155,500 with the loan currently in place. However, that figure reduces to $38,000 with a new loan at market rates. That's a massive delta, and, honestly, the difference between the investment making sense or not.

The story of convincing that bank to work with us is a memorable one. Let's just say it started rough ... as they couldn't quite understand why I thought they would hand over favorable lending terms to some random dude calling in from California. Loan assumptions were possible, they informed me, but the bank had full right to approve or deny based on their opinion of the new buyer.

It took some very creative deal structuring to satisfy the banks and enable the seller's "cheap money" to be transferred to us. I'll explain that move in just a moment. But first, let's review how this deal expanded from 108 units to 216 units the following day.

The Oaks

As Greg and I worked through the initial conversations with the bank, we received another phone call from the broker. He said the seller had an idea—since we stated in our video that we desired to buy more than one property in Des Moines—would we be interested in buying another 108-unit community that VareCo had recently purchased and secured crazy cheap financing for?

I'll be honest with you. I didn't see this coming, and at the moment, it seemed a bit overwhelming. I was happy taking down a sizable asset in a new market and "figuring it out." However, this journey was all about playing big and "doing what I would if I wasn't afraid." So I said yes, we told him to send the details on the other property, and we'd see if we could make the whole thing work.

The Oaks was just a mile from the first property and technically the "better" of the two assets long term, but it was in rough shape. The prior owner had let it go, and there was a big repositioning that needed to happen. On the financing side, the property had a loan out for $5M with a 3.3% fixed interest rate. The difference in annual debt service between this and a potential replacement loan was even more striking than the first property.

What's more—purchasing two sites this close to one another gave us immediate access to a lot of advantages of scale that we reviewed in the last chapter. We would be able to save on staffing and management costs, and could cross-sell the properties to prospective renters, which would get more leases signed. Scale helped our investors too. With two properties, we have optionality in terms of our long-term holding and cash management strategy.

Looking back, this decision to double the size of our first deal in Des Moines ended up being the pivotal moment for us as it changed the scope of the conversation. This was no longer a simple purchase but a significant partnership in the making. That's because the bank handling this property had the same objections as the first bank. They were not going to hand over this loan easily. It was time to get really creative.

Meeting Requirements

Although the requirements vary by lender and by mortgage product, here's a simple rule to keep in mind. Any bank you approach for a commercial loan is going to want to see your personal net worth equal or exceed the balance of the loan you are applying for.

Soooo, for DSM1, that meant I needed to show a net worth of $10M. (Many banks exclude personal homes and retirement accounts, by the way.) I'm not here to put my personal balance sheet on display, but I can tell you it did not equal

$10M at the time of this purchase. And that created a major issue.

But like all things in business and finance, there are workarounds. The term "key principals" (KP) as written into our plan refers to a type of capital partner that brings balance sheet wealth (read: bank statements) to the loan application. Doing so allows the "borrower," who can be a collection of people, to check the proper box with bank underwriters.

I knew this coming in, and we had identified a few individuals who had stated they would be willing to KP for us. However, verbally stating support and signing on the line for a $10M liability are two very different things. As we thought through our options it hit us—these loans already had a KP. The current borrower!

The answer was to keep the seller "on the loan" after the sale. By doing so, we removed the barrier that was preventing the assignment. Amazingly, this was an easy decision for Terrance and his team. He loved the assets and had bought them for a reason—he believed their value would continue increasing over time. VareCo was also motivated to keep their team intact as selling off this many units would likely cause them to downsize their local property management team.

DSM1

In the end, it was all about aligning interests. It took about two weeks to sort everything out regarding the terms of our agreement. Through very open communication and a long,

in-person dinner, we landed on an arrangement that got both
parties excited.

Greg and I created a new entity called DSM1 LLC, which
serves to consolidate funds and hold the title of the properties.
It really was a win-win.

Measured Capital got control of 216 units of multifamily
real estate in our target market of Des Moines and two assets
that had big upside. This was the beachhead we needed to
jumpstart our business.

VareCo got to recognize a profit on the low cost-basis they
secured, but liked the future prospects of the assets so much
that they wanted to stay in the deal. Terrance and his brother
Danny, who leads the team and operations in Des Moines,
continued on as co-managers with us and put in a significant
amount of their own capital to the holding entity as well.

In a final twist, by working together, we actually got the
banks to increase the amount they were lending, and both
added second mortgages on top of the existing ones. In the
end, we bought two properties for $16.5M and had banks
provide over $12M in funding.

With that, I bring you to the punchline of this chapter and
the biggest lesson from our first big deal as lead sponsors:

The bank is my biggest investor.

It should be yours as well.

I see so many new investors get worked up about how to raise equity to fund acquisitions. Meanwhile, they take banks for granted and just pencil in some number for the loan amount. I see this as a huge mistake and a wasted opportunity that I want to help you avoid.

Before moving into the theory and application of debt to your investing business, let's first review our "napkin plan" above and see how we did.

Napkin Plan Audit

Looking back to the five-point "napkin plan" that got this game started—these assets fit all the criteria of points one and two. The location, size, and age of the buildings were exactly as expected. Points three and five were also on track—the deal was a bit larger and it took a month longer than forecasted, but we'll take that combo any day.

That leaves us with point four of the "napkin plan," the point about the key principals. I focus on it here because not many people talk about it. It really doesn't become an issue until, well, until you try to take out a loan for $10M. And you learn that the bank has no interest in giving you $10M. And then you conclude this whole private investing thing is too hard and the system is rigged and all the rest of the victim stories I often hear by folks who aren't educated on this process.

Instead, let's get confident and learn how to play the game so we can access the largest and cheapest pool of capital available to any investor.

Good Debt, Bad Debt

In my 20s, I picked up a copy of a book with a purple cover that forever changed my perspective on money and wealth. It's called *Rich Dad, Poor Dad*, and it has inspired many individuals who today find themselves financially free and "working" as full-time investors. Early in the book, the author Robert Kiyosaki introduces the idea of debt being good in some situations while it can be bad in others.

Let's use two transactions that happen every day to illustrate the difference. Example one: buying a big screen TV on a credit card with a 17% interest rate and no cash in your bank account to pay the credit card bill that will come due 30 days later. That is bad debt. Example two: buying an investment asset that creates 8% cash-flow returns and using a 5% fixed rate mortgage to pay for two-thirds of the purchase price. That is good debt. Actually, no it's not. That is great debt.

It's great debt because not only have we acquired and gained control of a bigger asset and stream of income than we paid for in cash; we're also earning more income from the financed portion of the asset than we are paying in expenses to control it. This is so different from example one and the negative debt situations many Americans find themselves in; it's hard to think that both can be lumped into the same category.

Understanding this differentiation from Kiyosaki is fundamental. Summarizing his theory—good debt is borrowing that leads to the acquisition of income-producing assets, which has the effect of building wealth over time. Bad debt is borrowing that leads to buying of consumables or depreciating assets like cars and electronics, which has the effect of reducing wealth over time.

Commercial vs. Residential Loans

An important place to start when understanding commercial real estate loans is that they function the same and serve the same purpose as traditional mortgages taken out to purchase single-family homes, yet have a totally different set of rules and standards. This source of money is also accessed through totally different channels and with companies that many traditional investors have never heard of.

There are two main differences between a home loan and an apartment loan that really surprise people. And yes—both points make the commercial version harder to calculate and more difficult to understand. However, they really can serve the investor better when applied correctly.

Loan Term

The term of a loan, or simply, the length of time required to repay the loan, is the first major difference. Commercial loans have much shorter terms than traditional home mortgages, and this reality has some serious consequences to the borrower.

The standard term of a residential mortgage is 30 years. Most feature a 30-year pay-down schedule, also known as "amortization period," meaning the loan balance is being reduced to zero with the last mortgage payment.

The standard term of a commercial mortgage is five to seven years. Most also feature amortization periods of 25 or 30 years, meaning the loan balance will definitely *not* be paid off with the last payment. Somewhere between 80% to 90%

of the original balance will remain. The end of nearly all commercial loan terms is met with a balloon payment, which is the bank saying, "Pay me back the remaining balance … now." Due to the way amortization works, very little principal balance gets paid over the first five years of a loan, which introduces the need for frequent refinancing to any commercial real estate asset.

Yes, this whole industry is built on the assumption that every dollar of debt issued for these properties will be recycled back within about seven years. This was crazy to me at first. Coming from single-family homes where I always had the assumption that loans were issued specifically for the reason of paying off the asset and owning it outright long term. I had dreams of 20 homes all paid off in my retirement, creating a great life for my wife and me. Then I realized that I had taken out nine home mortgages in my life, all with 30-year terms, and the longest one I had held was—wait for it—seven years. The average was 4.5.

Refinancing is a part of life as a professional investor. Veteran investors know they will be financing and refinancing their assets indefinitely. It's the most efficient way to deploy capital. As we will show with some amazing math later, it is usually well worth the effort to all parties to refresh loan terms every five to seven years.

Loan Size

The other major assumption in residential loans that does not carry over to commercial lending is the size of loans. This is commonly expressed with the term loan-to-value (LTV).

This metric shows how much of the purchase price the bank is going to finance.

The residential lending market has been standardized on 80% LTV since the 1950s and the creation of the Federal Housing Administration's mortgage insurance program. That leaves only 20% of the price, the down payment, that must be provided in cash by the buyer. It's been this way since I first heard the word "mortgage," and due to government policy and institutions, it will likely stay that way for a very long time.

The commercial lending market has no standard LTV although it averages around 65%. This is significant, as it requires buyers to bring much larger down payments to acquire these properties. The reason for this is straightforward—there is far less policy and government insurance behind commercial loans, meaning the issuing lenders often have to take significant losses if a borrower defaults. Hence, because commercial banks really care about getting their money back, they judge the risk of these loans to be higher and, therefore, pull back the amount they lend. The lower the LTV, the easier it will be for a lender to foreclose and get their principal back in the event of the borrower defaulting.

There are a number of formulas and standards that banks use to "size" these loans. The underlying idea behind all of them is that they judge the property's ability to pay back the loan, not the borrower's. Yes, they will underwrite the borrower and ensure that person is in good financial shape before approving a loan, but their main concern is the property and its potential to generate enough income to pay for the interest bill that arrives each month.

How much income does it make today? How much do comparable properties produce? Where is it located, and what's happening around there? What history does this borrower have increasing rents and income over time?

Those, along with many other questions in a similar line, will dictate how much "proceeds" or dollars will be issued upon approval of the loan.

Please visit the Appendix for more details on what I see as some very important terms for you to learn, so you can speak the language of commercial lending.

Leveraging Leverage

This chapter has been all about using the commercial credit markets to reduce risk and amplify the returns of owning income-producing assets. I'd like to share two final concepts that I've learned through my journey that are now important parts of my everyday thinking as an investment sponsor that should serve you as well.

Positive Leverage

Leverage, in its most basic form, can be likened to using a seesaw to lift a heavy object. By applying a small force on one end, you can lift a much heavier weight at the other end. This principle of using minimal effort to achieve a greater result permeates many aspects of life, not just finance.

In the context of real estate investing, there is a concept known as "positive leverage" that takes this a step further. It occurs when we not only use less money to buy through borrowing, but the returns on the purchased asset actually exceed the cost of the debt. For example, if you purchase a property with a mortgage and the rental income from the property produces a higher yield-on-cost than the interest rate on the debt, you're effectively making a profit on money that was never yours in the first place. This creates a form of positive arbitrage, amplifying an investment's efficiency and reducing financial risk in acquiring large assets. This is a strategy that savvy investors use to tilt the scales in their favor, enabling them to wager millions of dollars of capital with confidence.

Liquidity

Liquidity refers to how quickly and easily an asset can be converted into cash without significantly affecting its price. In real estate, while owning income-producing assets is crucial, there are times when converting these assets back into liquid cash becomes necessary.

Consider the example of a real estate investor who owns several properties free and clear. The properties generate rental income, which is excellent, but the investor might find themselves needing a large sum of cash for new opportunities or unexpected expenses. Here, refinancing becomes a powerful tool. By taking out new loans against the properties, the investor can extract cash from the equity built up over time.

This process doesn't just provide the necessary funds but does so while allowing the person to retain ownership of the assets and continue to earn income from them. Refinancing for liquidity purposes is akin to an artist selling prints instead of the original painting; it allows the owner to capitalize on the asset's value repeatedly, maximizing financial flexibility and securing capital for further investments or other financial needs.

Shake Hands with the Bank

Most amateur investors complain about banks, the rigidity of lending and all the related paperwork and restrictions. In contrast, most professional investors love their lenders and the incredible leverage they get from their banking relationships.

Personally, I'm fascinated by banks, bankers, and the whole credit industry. Like compounding interest from the last chapter, it's not intuitive to most people how powerful and significant credit markets are to their lives. I've slowly gained an appreciation for this over my years of actively investing. I follow my interest with a lot of curiosity that has helped me understand the interests and main concerns of all bankers. Based on these conversations and experience, below is my guide to succeeding with banks.

1. **Be and act like a professional.** Yes, banks can be buttoned-up and stuffy, so when in Rome …! People fail with banks because they refuse to play the game. Do you want cheap money or not? Treat them as an investor in your projects. Just as you would prepare to pitch to a potential partner, approach bankers in the same way. This not only shows respect but also builds trust and professional rapport.

2. **Show up prepared.** Any dealings with a lender will involve lots of paperwork and forms. Many of them are standardized and can be anticipated. Personal financial

statements, statement of real estate owned, tax returns, and bank statements are four you can be assured of. So, get them ready, have them in a folder, and send them the moment the bank asks for them. If buying a property, they will need the current financial statements, the rent roll, and the tax records to even start the process, so deliver that before they ask! Come prepared, know your stuff, and you'll not only impress but expedite the entire process.

3. **Do their job for them**. Take it a step further and prepare the calculations they will need to do. Provide your full analysis, and save a copy that answers all the bank's questions. Greg and I have added lots of metrics to our underwriting package, so it's all there for them. Want to know expected cash flows after rents have stabilized in year four? Just click on the annual forecast tab and scroll to the bottom; it's right there. Go get the insurance quote, and stick that in the folder too. Save a copy of any pitch deck you may have prepared for yourself or investors, and reduce it to the essentials for the bankers. Include photos, tell the story. All of that matters! Understand their interests, align with them, and make their decision-making process as smooth as possible.

4. **Understand the bank's goals** and that they are very different from your own. Seek to understand, ask them questions about how it works on their side. I've done this hundreds of times, and I've learned one very clear thing. Let this be said, and let this be written: the only thing a bank actually cares about is getting paid back. The volume of loans and credit spreads a bank is booking don't matter if it experiences too much default and loses

its customers' money. One lost loan could wipe out 50 to 100 performing loans. So don't tell them how awesome this deal will be for you or your investors. Just show them how they will be paid back.

5. **Be the best borrower.** From application to servicing, just be the best customer the bank could ask for. Play the damn game. They are highly regulated and perform magic with money. It's stuffy and procedural, and it always will be. Do all of the above items, and do them in every interaction. Treat them like a customer. Build relationships, and earn trust. Be so good they tell stories about you to their peers at other banks and lending institutions.

Never Lose a Building

As part of Greg and my continued effort on our individual 100 Coffee Campaigns, we sometimes get access to some legendary investors. For me, that's guys and gals that have been active investors buying serious assets for 25-plus years and have achieved all their financial goals and more.

One such meeting occurred with a local sponsor that has been buying and holding apartments in Southern California for over 50 years. He has traded thousands of doors and has maintained a patient and long-term perspective throughout his career. He has also created big returns for some people we know locally that have invested in his deals.

As we spent a few hours swapping stories about our families, our careers, and, of course, investing in apartments, I eagerly wrote down snippets of wisdom. He had endless examples and case studies for every topic we reviewed. It was really inspiring. As our time came to an end, I asked for his best advice: "After all these years, what's the one thing you would tell your younger self?"

"Never lose a building."

"Never lose a building?"

"That's right."

Forty-year-old Dan looks at 80-year-old legend with total disappointment. I was certainly hoping for more. Being a savvy communicator, he picked up on my body language.

"Yes, never lose a building, Dan. I bet you plan on using debt, don't you? Just make sure you never put yourself in a position where you could lose a building to the lender. That's how investors get crushed and careers end. And that rule is why I'm still standing 50 years later."

Alrighty then. Never lose a building.

His message boils down to being reasonable with debt and never taking on so much or with such burdensome terms that it puts the investment at risk. Using a term from the Appendix, holding a long-term building with a DSCR of 0.8x isn't going to work out very well. Investors will be contributing new cash every month just to hold on to the place.

Like all areas of life—too much of anything can be a bad thing; but with moderation you can find balance by using good judgment and not get carried away. My rules for keeping debt moderate include using reasonable LTV, such as 65%, and always securing fixed interest rates so that future payments are known. Both of these will keep you in safer territory and massively increase the chances that you'll "never lose a building."

Mastering the Lending Landscape

In this chapter, we've navigated the intricate world of commercial loans, uncovering the pivotal role they play in transforming real estate ventures. By understanding and strategically employing loans, we've seen how they do much more than simply reduce initial capital outlay; they magnify the overall returns and open doors to substantial real estate opportunities.

As we transition to the next chapter, we will build on these foundations, focusing on cultivating the acumen required to act, think, and invest as sophisticated investors.

CHAPTER 12

Capital vs. Money

The Ramsey Show is a popular call-in radio broadcast that is live on the air every weekday for three hours. It fields inquiries from callers and offers financial advice—most of it centered around getting people out of debt. Its founder and core personality, Dave Ramsey, has been hosting this show for 32 consecutive years. In the process, he's written multiple books and developed a large business around his proprietary "debt snowball method" along with other resources for individuals looking to solve their personal money problems.

This show and its related tools claim to have helped upwards of ten million people to improve their financial situations. It doesn't take but a few minutes listening to the show or reading the books to understand his core message—debt is evil. When recommending a path forward to someone deep in credit card debt, Ramsey will establish an emotional and spiritual connection to money, offering guidance rooted in his belief that debt collectors are fundamentally dishonest, or "scum," as he often labels them.

This method has proven very effective, as it shifts the caller's perspective. Prior to the call, these individuals had been approaching their situation as a victim—taken advantage of by the big, bad financial industry. By vilifying debt and those who issue it, he gives his callers confidence and encourages them to stop playing the victim.

However—while Ramsey's advice is great for his target audience, it's downright foolish when applied to a different financial situation. It completely ignores basic economic concepts and overgeneralizes credit and money. For anyone who has proven responsible in money management and out-earns their spending habits, the total avoidance of debt and leverage is misapplied.

I share this view not to criticize Ramsey or his followers, but rather to point out the importance of aligning investor goals with investment philosophy. If someone is deep in credit card debt, then Ramsey is right, they should not be thinking about how to attain $3M in leverage from a commercial real estate lender. However, if you pay your credit card bill each month, earn a healthy wage, and fully fund your retirement account each year, then staying small isn't going to serve you. There are smarter ways to play this game and have a lot more fun doing it. Avoiding sophisticated investments just because they are harder to understand is the action of an amateur.

Turning Pro

The opposite of an amateur is a professional. And professionals don't shy away from powerful tools just because other people have misused those tools in the past. No, professionals double-down on their education and become experts in the tools of their craft. Professionals study other professionals, hire coaches, and develop discipline around their routines.

In 2021, after deciding to break out of my High Achievement Trap, I was on a mission to become a professional investor. I was an investor, possibly even qualifying for "sophisticated" status given my experience, but I was not yet a professional.

For my birthday that year, a good friend of mine handed me a copy of a book that would forever change my perspective on this topic. It's called *Turning Pro* by Steven Pressfield, and it reminded me that this shift from amateur to professional is not just about what I'm doing, but about how I'm thinking and being.

Becoming a professional is more about the mindset we adopt and the beliefs that drive our decisions. So, to increase my chances of making this shift, I looked to the wisdom of my growing community of peers and supporters. Just like I mentioned in previous chapters, I utilized the 100 Coffee Campaign as a way to get in front of a lot of smart and sophisticated investors. That is when I realized I was meeting with two different types of people—financial amateurs and investment pros. And it was abundantly clear that those individuals and families who truly turned pro financially understand that *money is different from capital*.

Capital vs. Money

Before these interactions and the insight I gained from them, money was money. I had studied the word "capital" in business school and understood that, in an economic sense, it referred to assets that increase productivity or create financial returns. However, I had never really applied it to my own life. For some reason, I thought of capital as a business concept and all personal wealth as just money. But when I sat across from guys and gals that had achieved financial freedom through ownership of income-producing assets, it was clear they had both and treated the two very differently.

Money is for spending, for buying goods and services, and for increasing the quality of life we experience. When we treat a dollar as money, we understand that it will flow away from us and not return, having the effect of reducing our net wealth.

Capital, on the other hand, is for investing, for buying income-producing assets and for creating future streams of passive cash flows. When we treat a dollar as capital, we understand that it will attract other dollars to flow towards us, having the effect of increasing our net worth.

This idea seems so simple, yet requires huge mental discipline to adhere to over the long term. And that is what professional and sophisticated investors showcase when they keep capital and money separate in their minds. They don't confuse the two, and they don't mix the two. They have clear rules around how their money is managed and how frequently it is converted to capital.

Besides directing resources into wealth-producing activities, this mental framework also provides these investors a sense of calm. Their disciplined and professional approach means they don't need to stress when they spend money. They have designated a certain amount as "money" (as opposed to "capital") to be spent, and they do so confidently, without any hesitation or regrets.

Amateurs get themselves into trouble by mixing these two categories of financial currency. They build a savings account with the intent that it will work as capital, but life and the desire for a new kitchen get in the way, and this potential capital goes out to pay for personal expenses. In the process, it is converted back to money, and this lack of discipline keeps these individuals stuck in their High Achievement Traps.

While on this topic of money and capital and currency, I'd like to share another idea that informs the investment thesis of many professional investors.

The Money Supply

In any sovereign economic system, there is an agreed-upon currency which all participants use to exchange value. One such system is the United States' economy, and we have all agreed to use the dollar as our shared currency. Everyone in the system understands that the dollars in their wallet and showing in their bank account is the official currency. In the US, the amount of currency in circulation, or the money supply, is controlled by the central bank, the Federal Reserve (the Fed). This institution measures the supply of money with two metrics, M1, which represents all liquid forms of money like physical currency and check deposits, and M2, which includes all items in M1, plus savings deposits and short-term securities.

The fascinating thing about the money supply, and why it matters in a chapter about being a professional investor, is that it is always expanding. This growth in the amount of currency in the system is inherent to the theory of modern economics. Growth is necessary for capitalism to work, and that's the system we are all playing in right now. Ironically, we actually just went through the first significant reduction to M2 since the Fed started making records, but that was only in response to the absurd expansion of M2 as a result of government stimulus à la COVID-19. Even with these reductions, the total supply is up 25% between 2020 and 2023.

And what happens when we constantly expand the amount of currency in its system? We get inflation. Again, this is inherent and necessary to current macroeconomics. A small amount of inflation is actually a good thing, and the goal of the Fed is to keep our system expanding at 2% per year. Sometimes it's less, and we get deflation, sometimes we get more and have high inflation, but over the long term, we see growth.

This short economics lesson is valuable, as it has massive implications to your investment strategy and understanding this idea of capital vs money. It is vital to the mitigation of risk when deploying capital to create future income.

Today and Yesterday

When you buy a hard asset like an apartment building, you do so in today's dollars. Today is whatever date you make the purchase and the moment on the money supply chart where you enter the game. All things kept equal, the value of the asset you purchase will follow the money supply up over time. The rents you charge in five years, however, will be in tomorrow's dollar and wherever the money supply happens to be in five years from now. Same idea if you decide to sell the building, it will be done in tomorrow's dollars (yet, your cost basis and any debt balance remains in what are now "yesterday's" dollars).

This is the case for all hard assets and is a major reason wealthy individuals buy lots of hard assets with their capital. They do really well in inflationary environments. And if we take a long-term perspective, then we are always in an inflationary environment.

Meanwhile, the debt that you take out will be priced in the dollars of today, the day you book the loan. Paying that loan payment, however, will happen with tomorrow's dollars. That debt remains denominated in today's currency while you pay it off with income that comes from tomorrow's currency, when there could be twice as much of it in circulation. This is time-based arbitrage that all amateur investors seem to miss.

A final way to drive home the impact of an expanding money supply to a disciplined investor that keeps capital working long term is with the idea of "replacement cost." The materials and labor used to construct buildings become more expensive every year. That means tomorrow's buildings will cost more to build than yesterday's. This doesn't have a huge impact over two or three years, but expand to 25 years and historical materials and labor seem impossibly cheap. Buying existing assets "below replacement cost" is an important metric for buildings that were built before the turn of the century.

Capital Allocation and Patience

Another clear separation between investment amateurs and professionals is in the way they allocate capital. Along with their mental discipline to keep capital and money separate, the most successful investors also put their capital into very different assets than beginners.

Check out the reports issued by Forbes, Bloomberg, or the like, and it's clear that the world's wealthiest people put a vast majority of their investment capital in two types of income-producing assets: commercial real estate and operating businesses. Both are held through a legal structure referred to as "private equity" with the exception of those whose wealth came from taking a private company public and, therefore, shifting the classification of their wealth.

There is a high-net-worth peer network called "Tiger 21" that connects and provides investing information to its members. Its hallmark report is the quarterly Asset Allocation Report. I've been receiving this for a few years now, and it always confirms that the more wealthy someone is, the higher percentage of their wealth is held in private equity investments. In fact, by the time we get to billionaires—it's upward of 90%.

Folks, if holding shares in a diversified basket of publicly traded companies was the best way to build and protect their wealth, billionaires would own nothing but stocks. But they don't. They own *some* stocks and bonds and the like. There are clear advantages to putting some portion of wealth to this market. But they own way more private equity investments. And those investments are often holding companies for a specialized type of commercial business or commercial real estate.

A final point on what we can take from the most successful investors is patience. In Chapter 10, I shared a story about how 99% of Warren Buffet's wealth can be attributed to nothing more than his patience. He's considered the greatest investor the world has ever seen, and his formula is very clear: allocate capital to income-producing assets and wait.

Relationship with Money

At the end of the day, this topic is all about your relationship with money.

By spending time with veteran investors, I learned the blueprint for becoming a professional investor. I invite you to follow this plan as well.

By surrounding yourself with peers, mentors, coaches, and people who have achieved what you are looking to achieve, I believe you'll see firsthand how some individuals have changed their relationship to the almighty dollar.

A huge piece of investing success is how consistently we can follow our own rules about how, when, why, and where to allocate currency from our bank accounts and turn it into investment capital that eventually provides the freedom we're aiming for.

Good capital is patient. Good capital is long term. Good capital is aligned with the goals, timelines, and risk profile of the projects it's invested in.

Owners of good capital are educated on their strategies and look for situations where the deck is stacked in their favor. Those topics will be our focus moving forward. In the next and final section of this book, we move into the active functions of investing in private real estate deals. I'll continue to share the best lessons I've learned as I made the commitment to turning pro and quickly went from 200 units to 900 units over the following 12 months.

PART 3 INVEST

*The "Invest" stage is where we deploy our time and money to achieve the goals we've set and live into our vision of a bigger future. This is about **becoming** an investor, not just doing the act of investing or getting the result.*

CHAPTER 13

Un-Level the Playing Field

Within a few months of closing on the properties in DSM1, Greg and I felt comfortable with the direction of that project and the team managing it on-site. Occupancy was on the rise, net income grew each month, and our construction efforts were physically transforming the site. The performance of the project gave Greg and me the confidence to expand our efforts—it was time to start looking for our next deal.

The only problem was that the commercial real estate market was melting down around the country at that time. It was still early 2023 and the impact of the Federal Reserve's series of aggressive interest rate hikes had begun to take its toll on the nation's property market. In the 12 months preceding March of that year, the Fed funds rate had moved from 0.5% to 4.5% (a 900% increase!) with reports and communication making it clear that more hikes were on the way.

This caused quite the shift in industry sentiment. Just six months prior, the market for apartment acquisitions was red hot, and deals were being bid up by multiple aggressive offers and nonrefundable deposits. Now, since it was becoming clear that the near future would be challenging for credit markets, real estate investors were starting to "put their pencils down" regarding new deals and take a look at their current portfolios.

Looking back, the reports would later reveal that some markets experienced an 80% reduction in transaction volumes by the second quarter of 2023.

Meanwhile, Greg and I continued with our Coffee Campaigns. We agreed that the most important thing to our business, the one thing that made everything easier or unnecessary, was continuing to build relationships with potential capital partners, brokers, and anyone else who could help us build a portfolio long term. We entered the year with great energy and huge visions. However, within a few months of meetings with freaked-out investors and deep-in-trouble sponsors, their pessimism started to rub off on us. Everyone kept telling us that "no deals are getting done right now," and slowly I allowed myself to adopt this belief.

One day in April, I sat down with my mentor, Vance, and gave him an update on the status of our business and the big shift occurring in my life. Vance had been instrumental in directing my focus and supporting my move to playing bigger. His body language in response to my update was troubling. I knew the look on his face when he was hearing someone he cared about share limiting beliefs. After five minutes of me giving details and examples of how challenging things were, he responded with the following:

"I don't know if that view is going to serve you very well, Dan. I just met with another real estate investor yesterday, and they've completed two big purchases just this month."

And he was right—even if transaction volume was down 80%, that still meant 20% of deals were happening. Someone was closing. Why couldn't it be me?

This was the push I needed. Greg and I met a few times that week to double-down on our conviction. We had selected this path and asset class for a reason, and we still believed in the fundamentals long term, so we massively increased our activity. We flew to Des Moines, Jacksonville, and Waco to meet with every broker in those markets and toured every deal that could possibly fit our buy box.

The visits to Jacksonville and Waco created some momentum but were fruitless in terms of finding viable opportunities. We were still unknown in those markets, and the brokers had good reason to not take us seriously for the size of deal we were pursuing. We had no proven track record in their market, and this prevented us from "showing" what we were capable of.

In Des Moines, however, we found a warmer reception. That is because, for months, we retained the distinction of completing the "largest recent real estate transaction" in the market. And because of who we partnered with and how we had structured our first deal, the brokers started to take us seriously. But I learned the difference between being a capable buyer and one that has a clear competitive advantage. Our next story shows how this works firsthand.

Beat 'Em or Join 'Em

While Greg and I were complaining about the challenges in the commercial real estate market and obstacles we saw preventing our second deal from happening, some other investors were gathering in Las Vegas at an event put on by the National Multifamily Housing Council (NMHC) to discuss the few deals that could be coming up for sale in the following year.

Two of those in attendance were Terrance and Danny—the guys we had just bought The Jefferson and The Oaks from. We'd been communicating with them on a weekly basis as we executed the business plan of our shared investment in DSM1. During the event, they learned of two communities with 54 units each on the northeast side of Des Moines that would need to be sold in the coming year.

The buildings had quite the backstory. Their long-term owner had sold them to his maintenance guy. However, the maintenance guy didn't know how to operate 100-plus apartment units, so he defaulted and gave the property back. To make matters worse, the buildings had existing bank debt with a heavy prepayment penalty, meaning the owner couldn't exit the loan upon sale without paying a massive sum to the bank (remember, commercial loans are complicated).

Shortly after the NMHC conference, we were contacted by a broker who got wind of this opportunity and thought to pull us in as potential buyers. While explaining to us what he knew, he mentioned that our friends at VareCo were interested as well. In fact, Danny had toured the properties a few days prior.

It was here that we found ourselves at a crossroad. As our operating partners, we were highly impressed with how Terrance and Danny worked. Their energy and integrity were clear to us; and the more we talked, the more we recognized we shared the same long-term vision. All four of us held nearly the exact same thesis about rental assets in the Des Moines market and were committed to acquiring a door count into the thousands. However, Des Moines is also a small market with limited deal flow.

That's when Greg and I realized we had a decision to make— we were either going to compete with them or join forces. And by my calculations, competing was going to be difficult. They had been buying in this market for ten years and had meaningful relationships with most of the brokers and bankers in town.

Once we connected with Terrance and talked about the deal in more detail, we learned that Danny loved the upside it presented and was dead set on buying it. As it turned out, both of them had been thinking that this could be a perfect opportunity to partner with us as well.

DSM2

The weeks that followed presented a masterclass in leveraging each other's strengths to gain and apply a competitive advantage to not only win this challenging deal, but create a business plan and capital stack (the mix of debt and equity sources) that is set up for success. After discussing what each of us needed to do and agreeing to the project forecasts, VareCo and Measured Capital entered into a legally binding two-party joint venture agreement. It clarified each party's role, responsibility, risks, and rewards if certain things were to occur within the investment holding period.

Terrance led the charge securing the deal and negotiating the best terms possible. To address the seller's mortgage prepayment issue, we presented an arrangement where he would carry back 80% of the purchase price as a seller-financed loan. This allowed him to keep the current mortgage in place and collect income, but still sell the asset and move title and to our control. This arrangement had a six-year term, plenty for us to stabilize the properties and either sell or refinance at a higher valuation.

Danny focused on the physical asset, renovation improvements, deferred maintenance, due diligence, and preparation of the property management team. Greg focused on the underwriting model and further developing the business plan. He also prepared our official five-year profit and loss forecast—having considered all the data we needed to be confident to execute on this $8M-plus purchase.

For me, I continued to focus on doing what I had learned to do best: figure out where the capital is going to come from. A new deal meant the chance to get in front of more private investors who were looking for this kind of asset. A new entity named "DSM2 LLC" was created to hold the properties, take out the mortgages, and consolidate investor funds.

As I reviewed the whole situation in my mind the night after closing, I began to realize what it really meant to have a clear competitive advantage, to be the preferred buyer, and the value of being able to lock up a deal and figure out the details afterwards. Let's continue now by exploring some of those specific advantages and see how you can put them to work in the execution of your thesis.

Advantages at Work

The experience above was an early teacher on the power of developing a clear competitive advantage in an investing business. In fact, to play this game at a high level, it is absolutely necessary. I would argue that it's very risky to invest without one (or many!). On the contrary, some investors develop such an edge that they can remove a large amount of risk from their deals. In the case study above, Greg and I benefited greatly by positioning ourselves on the same team as two established investors who had already accrued a number of clear advantages.

The first and most obvious advantage was insider knowledge of the market. Terrance and his team had access to information not available to outsiders. For example, most investors go to CoStar or perform market research to figure out what rents could be charged after improving a property. Danny knows the rent roll for many of his current properties off the top of his head and could call his leasing managers for more details. They could tell him exactly what rents they could get and even describe a target renter. He had a pulse for every submarket in town and even what owners would likely be selling in the near future.

Another advantage at work was the existing economies of scale. These two had built high-performing property management teams that specialized by function—leasing, collections, maintenance, construction, etc. When a new property was acquired, those teams could get some new units to manage and likely add a team member to handle the additional volume. No need for custom processes or reinventing the wheel; it was rinse and repeat.

The final advantage I saw move the needle was reputation and relationships. Like most industries, this business is all about relationships. People do business with people they like and trust. And trust takes time to build.

All of the above combined into a massive advantage in our market to (1) lock up a great opportunity with limited competition, (2) have the confidence in our underwriting and business plan, and (3) leverage relationships to change the terms of the transaction massively in our favor. This is stacking the deck.

Developing Your Advantage

As seen through the stories above, advantages accrue to investors exactly when and where you expect them to develop—around the unique strengths of individual investors and through their direct focused effort. In other words, these things don't happen randomly. The commercial real estate game is a very competitive space, and just like a football team that doesn't practice or know their playbook, an investor without an edge will get blown out by more sophisticated opponents that have been practicing and can execute like a professional.

To develop this capacity in your own investing, the best place to start is with your natural skills and personal interest. Are you the smartest, the most social, the most inquisitive, the most detailed, or the most tech savvy? Do you know something about a particular market, a particular street, a particular zip code? Do you have connections with influential people in a specific market? A rich uncle that would love to help you get started?

The most important part of developing an advantage is starting from somewhere that's clear and obvious to you. If you have to force it and become someone you are not, it's not going to work. Use your natural strengths and then lean into those. A great way to do this in practice is to purchase a copy of the book *StrengthsFinder* by Gallup and use its online assessment to get your unique answers. Once you know your top five strengths, ask how you could use those natural talents to drive results in real estate investing. The following chapters will begin to break down the key roles and responsibilities of a great principal investor or deal sponsor that you can live into.

At the end of the day, you'll need to be the best in class at something. Maybe it's nothing more than picking a sponsor and writing a check. You can be world class at that and make 15-plus percent annual returns for the rest of your life. Or maybe you're willing to roll up your sleeves and invest your own money and other people's at the same time. If so, the rewards will be even richer, but understand that you're signing up for a job. We'll talk about the roles that you could potentially play in Chapters 15 and 16. Let's finalize this by reviewing how to become best in class.

Best in Class

Over our first two years in business, Greg and I have come to recognize that our single best advantage in the marketplace is our unique partnerships with other high-performing and high-integrity operators and the leverage we achieve in the process. We knew upfront that we wouldn't be living in the markets we invested in, so having best-in-class "boots on the ground" was a top concern as we finalized our thesis and laid out the long-term strategy.

However, my approach wasn't just to find the best multifamily property management company, but rather to develop exclusive partnerships and custom arrangements with companies who were capable of being the best. We wanted property managers who had existing systems and scale but would treat our assets as if they owned them themselves. Playing to our strengths and backgrounds, we designed our agreements in a way that the property management company did, in fact, own a piece of the building and had their own capital at risk in the asset as well.

In Des Moines, we helped our partners improve their reporting and governance as they scaled to a dramatically larger unit count in 2023. They brought our deals on as their only assets owned by a third party, stress testing their internal systems and operations. In Jacksonville, we identified the best property management company in town, who also happens to be owned by some great friends that I invested with in the past. We worked to expand their footprint into larger multifamily assets. In both cases, as the first third-party client with hundreds of doors under management, we were patient with our partners as they expanded their capabilities around us, focusing on the outcomes we valued the most.

Of course, I don't share these examples to say this is the only way or even the best way. In fact, I share it for the opposite reason—to show that something as simple as "aligning with a property manager you really believe in" can be the advantage that helps you win deals and produce above-average returns.

It doesn't have to be novel. It doesn't have to be complicated. It's really just about determining the unique alignment for you and your goals to play on a bigger stage and gain access to more freedoms.

<u>Reaping the Rewards</u>

We can end this discussion with a firm reminder of how necessary gaining this edge can be. To be successful and move forward in living into your inspired visions, you'll want to develop this kind of distinctive edge that delivers exclusive and discounted deals that fit your criteria.

Then you'll have to develop a system to execute the plan better than others. As has been true for Greg and me, you might find that a special relationship with the best operating partner in a given market is a core strategy and can yield you this advantage.

The examples in this chapter serve to show you how competitive advantages work and how de-risking strategies come in so many varieties. From experience and hard knocks, or from innovation and creativity. To make this happen, you need to systemize this advantage. Write it down. Test it out and always be developing your competitive advantage!

In the next chapter, we'll take this advantage and turn it into a business plan that gives us confidence as we move into the unknown future.

CHAPTER 14

Forecasting the Future

Earlier I introduced you to my first sales manager, John, the former special forces officer who taught me many of the fundamentals of being a sales person and producer. After helping me narrow down my prospecting list and target market, I started opening accounts and booking sales. A few months later, my next major lesson was delivered. During my quarterly business review with John, he asked for my forecast for the upcoming month.

"Ummm, forecast?"

"Yeah, you've got accounts now. How much are they going to buy this month?"

Realizing I had never really considered that I could predict how much one customer would buy before the month even began, I buckled up for what was sure to be another one of his classic sales-is-like-war analogies.

A couple minutes later he was deep in a story about two wartime generals who handled their victories very differently. The first general raided his enemy's territory and looted its wealth, killed innocent people, and then ran off to the next city. The second general received a surrender from his enemy, let everyone but a few soldiers live, and then worked with the conquered people to rebuild while levying new taxes on them. Over time, that first general ran out of steam and ended up in an early grave while the second general ruled an empire. The punchline to this story was a phrase John then repeated hundreds of times during my tenure with that company: "Pigs get fat and hogs get slaughtered, Dan!" He then connected this seemingly random story to the topic at hand: "Just like your customers and forecast. A bunch of these yahoos you work with are always going for whale accounts and home-run deals. But they usually strike out. You don't need to hit home-runs to win at this game. Just grow a list of customers that transact with you on a regular basis. That's what will make you successful as a salesperson—consistency."

The lesson concluded, "You'll be a professional when you can confidently hand me a list of accounts and the amount of revenue they'll create in that month ... and then go out and do it."

The teacher had yet again changed the game with this simple story and lesson. The message was simple—be a pig, not a hog. In the story, hogs are greedy and lazy, they walk into the arena unprepared and just hope it all works out. Sometimes they get lucky and it does work out, but over time, a hog is like a gambling addict, continuing to play games where the odds are specifically against them. Pigs, on the other hand, are thoughtful and develop a plan before starting the game. They pick higher-odds situations and know how to recognize when they've been successful, so they can stop and enjoy the spoils of their efforts.

Before this talk, the first day of the month as a salesperson was terrifying. My number started at zero, and I honestly wasn't sure where the next sale would come from. After this conversation, I started each month by pulling a report of last month's sales, listed by customer, and then coming up with an activity plan to ensure I would be in front of those customers to earn their business again in the coming month.

The resulting document would be my forecast for the coming month. I'd share it with my manager and a few peers to hold myself accountable. It wasn't perfect, and some months had a big variance, but over time, my results started to come in at or above my targets nearly every month.

What a difference! The forecasting process had so many positive effects on me it's hard to document them all. I gained confidence because I had the data to show me the list of companies that were likely to buy from me that month. I found a sense of calm, as I had less anxiety about what the future would bring.

What's more, I became a better contributor to the company's success as my forecasts would inform the purchasing and operations team of upcoming volume; this allowed them to plan inventory and staff to deliver on whatever I was selling.

I gained new friends in the finance department and executive suite, the two areas in the company that other salespeople didn't dare to go to. Through these years of building a business, I gained a skill that has transferred to every other business endeavor that I've been a part of since.

But exactly how do you do a forecast in real estate investing? What is involved in becoming good at predicting the future?

Underwriting Is Forecasting

The exact concepts shared in the story above apply to making great decisions in investment real estate. In order to be confident in the pursuit of an asset and develop the kind of conviction needed to close on big deals, we need to do some forecasting of our own. In the banking and insurance world, this process is officially called "underwriting," and that is the term we use as real estate investors as well.

Underwriting is the process of evaluating the potential risks and returns associated with an investment opportunity. It will involve analyzing various factors such as the property's location, condition, market demand, income potential, and the expenses required to operate it. All of this goes to determine the investment's viability and profitability.

The process of underwriting is one of researching the past and forecasting the future. It involves digging into certain risk factors, so they can be understood and mitigated. The outcome is a financial model that shows a pro forma (fancy phrasing for "hypothetical") income statement and the effect on cash flows throughout the holding period. I dig into some specifics and share my recommended best practices with you later in this chapter.

Price vs. Value

In my life as a technology salesperson, I developed relationships with some customers that were absolute characters. One of my favorites was a former trader on the stock exchange in New York. He had a strong accent and threw a curse word into just about every sentence. When we negotiated the final prices of deals we were working together, he'd remind me of his favorite phrase:

"There's no such thing as bad merchandise … only bad prices."

I share this quote because it's so spot on, and I think about it frequently in my investing—if something checks all the boxes I set up as my criteria, and I'm an active investor on a mission to acquire a portfolio, then purchase decisions really just come down to price. By that, I mean that at a certain cost basis, I'd purchase every large apartment within the Des Moines or Jacksonville city limits. And my skills as an underwriter (read: financial future predictor) enable me to find that magic number. Of course, that number might not be seen as reasonable to others, but knowing it and sticking to it is why this whole process is worthwhile.

An important note is that there is no such thing as "correct" underwriting. Different parties will perform underwriting on the same asset and get very different results. That's because you always get more of whatever you focus on and what risks you are most concerned about.

If you're the bank, your sole interest is the borrower's ability to pay back the loan on time and in full. If you're the insurance company, you're really only interested in your risks for large and total loss events at the property. And if you're the investor, you're crunching numbers to see what kind of returns are possible and what kind of margin for error is built into the deal.

On that note, the projections that an investor creates while preparing their underwriting become the long-term business plan. The pro forma income statement, just like the sales person's forecast, provides you with a roadmap and definition of success. An investor knows they are on track with a deal at the two-year mark because they can look back and see the original projections.

In essence, forecasting allows you to make predictions about the future, which in turn enables you to hold yourself accountable as you navigate the investment journey. By adhering to the underwriting guidelines and staying true to the initial forecasts, you can effectively manage your investment, secure funding, and learn how to structure deals with a blend of capital and debt.

Additionally, if, as an investor, you choose to raise capital from external sources, the underwriting and forecasts you present to your investors are what you are essentially committing to deliver. Investors rely on these projections to make informed decisions and to hold you accountable for the promises made. Therefore, accountability plays a crucial role in the underwriting process and throughout the lifecycle of the investment.

How to Underwrite

The process to underwrite commercial real estate isn't much different from creating a sales forecast. You collect historical data and mix in your research and knowledge of market conditions, current trends, and your team's ability to execute on a business plan.

First, before you spend any time analyzing a deal, let's start by announcing there is no need to spend time on properties that fall outside of your buy box and thesis. Let's refer to this as the "qualitative filter." Is it located in one of your target cities? Is it on a street you like and desire to own? Does it have the number of doors and vintage you require? If it does hit your buy box on all these basic levels, then it's time to get into the numbers.

I tend to think and approach underwriting in three different levels with each level requiring more time, effort, and resources, and each providing more detailed answers and sophisticated projections. Here's a quick explanation of each:

Level One: Seconds

First, there are the quick formulas and rules we can check in a matter of seconds. I can perform these quick formulas in my head and only need two or three basic data points. By running quick math on some big data points, I can determine if something is worthy of dedicating more of my time and effort to explore.

A great example of this is the One Percent Rule, introduced in Chapter One. A quick refresher: this rule states a property's monthly income per unit should exceed 1% of the purchase price. Just because a property passes this test does not automatically make it a good opportunity, and just because it fails the test, does not immediately eliminate it. However, it's a great measure of "how much a dollar of income costs to purchase," and a deal would require amazing opportunity in other areas if it didn't meet this standard. Other investors use the gross rent multiplier (GRM), which effectively tells us the same thing but uses annual income, which creates a slightly different scale. In both, the higher the number, the higher expected income will be coming along with the property.

Loss-to-lease (LTL) is another calculation we can do in our head with two data points that should be available at any time. This expresses how much rent is currently being left on the table. Take current rent and compare it to the market rent of a comparable property nearby. If there is a significant gap—say 20% or more—then there is likely some real value-add opportunity and chance to force serious appreciation if you can close the loss-to-lease gap after purchase.

Level Two: Minutes

The second level are frameworks that take minutes and benefit from a scratch piece of paper and a calculator. This is probably my personal sweet spot. Although I can do quick math and understand the big financial models in the next level, these focused calculations of important data early on help me save the most time and effort by not chasing deals I know will not work out.

Examples of this are figuring out the size of a loan that a property will qualify for while still walking the on-site tour. If you have the owner's claimed net operating income and you are aware of today's interest rates, then you can quickly determine how much debt the property can qualify for via some "back of the napkin" math. I love being able to do this because it enables me to "talk price" with conviction before I even break open a spreadsheet. I know that if I can't get 50% or more in proceeds given the seller's proposed price, it's likely not worth talking about.

Level Three: Hours

Finally, this third approach can easily consume hours. It involves Microsoft Excel, two monitors, a pair of headphones, and a quiet room. Just kidding, but I've been known to get obsessed about a particular building and do just that. I've also slapped together a model while making gross assumptions and being okay with a generalized output.

Regardless of how seriously you take it, this final level of underwriting is the official one, where you take a piece of software or a highly formulated and cross-referenced Excel file and input or modify hundreds of variables. These advanced models then take all these assumptions and produce forecasted financial statements and calculations on every kind of return metric you could hope for. Greg and I purchased a model specifically for multifamily assets that was being used by some peers in a mastermind group. We have since modified it so much that it is now called the Measured Underwriting Template (derived from the name of our company), and we are constantly making small tweaks as the metrics we concentrate on evolve.

My advice when it comes to this advanced and complete underwriting is to find a process and model that works for you and grow with it. There needs to be some level of proficiency, so you can get a sense of what the model is telling you. While we are on that topic, the single best thing you can do to improve your ability or skill in the area of underwriting and forecasting is to get reps!

Required Work

To be clear, this is not an optional activity. As the former stock trader's quote teaches us, underwriting is the activity that ensures you don't make a stupid mistake, like paying way too much for a certain building. To purchase an asset with the purpose of earning a return on that purchase requires you to be thorough and honest during this process. "I'm not good with numbers" or "Excel just isn't my thing" equates directly to "you're not going to be good at investing."

The best way to improve at this skill is to just do it. Set an activity goal for yourself. When I was getting started, my commitment was to take one deal per day through a complete underwriting process. Yes, it took hours, but I learned so much. I shared my results with peers and mentors, and I sent them to brokers and bankers for feedback.

I can't stress this communication part enough. Not only do we need to get reps, but it is imperative that we share our findings and see what others see. This is the only way to learn. Filling out spreadsheets in isolation won't get you there. Overall, the goal is simply to learn and get better at this essential skill because it's something you'll be doing over and over for any serious opportunity.

As you improve in this area, you will see its impact simplify your decision-making. By stress testing different scenarios, you can model how assets would perform under challenging conditions. What if occupancy dipped to 70%? What if you have a spike in utilities cost? What if a major mechanical system failed? What if you have the reserves and margin to pay for it?

Another reason that underwriting is required work is that it drives the due diligence checklist that is necessary to move a transaction through to closing. Although you should have a standard list that you bring to each deal, the process of underwriting creates questions, some of which are not easily answered until you have more access to information. And that access often doesn't come until after a PSA is signed and earnest money has been deposited. A great buyer will have their standard list as well as a list of unique items that came up while preparing the business plan and financial model.

Insurance is a good example of this. Although you can get preliminary quotes, insurance costs are often an estimate until well into the contract period. Details about the construction and age of certain systems is required; and it's just not feasible to access much of this prior to signing the PSA. Same goes for rents—when you do your analysis, you should always have an opinion of what potential rents will be for an asset in consideration. However, you should include "rent research" as part of your due diligence checklist and that includes driving the local neighborhoods and secret shopping all of the comparable properties in the area. This is work that is too time consuming for a deal that you aren't going to purchase but totally necessary if you are.

When I finish with a level three analysis and spend hours dissecting every line of income and expense, one thing is clear—I have confidence in my decision and conviction in my moves forward. And I derive that conviction through the idea that I feel confident in my forecast of what's most likely to happen.

What's Most Likely

One great American pastime that can teach us an important lesson on the topic of forecasting is fantasy football. Yes, the online game where adults "manage a team" by picking

NFL players and calculating points each week based on the performance of those players. Although I've given up the hobby to get my Sundays and attention back, one article I would always read to prepare for the draft to pick my roster is called the "Draft Day Manifesto" written by Matthew Berry. He's a humorous writer, so it's always an easy read, but I also loved his practical advice. The one big question he would pose to the reader before they stepped into their draft room is:

> *"What is most likely to happen?"*

Berry would encourage this question to be at the forefront of every decision during a draft. That's because, with 20 years of fantasy football data provided to him by his employer, ESPN, he understood that the winners of 95% of the millions of leagues he analyzed were those that simply played the odds. It wasn't the teams that picked the hot new rookie or breakout star. Because those outcomes were not likely to happen, they are pure speculation and have very poor results over the long-term.

It's the same thing as a casino. Any single hand could go your way, but stay for a few hours and the house's small edge will begin to show itself. And just like Berry's advice, the best real estate investors are those that create forecasts and underwriting models that are based on what is most likely to happen.

<u>Conclusion</u>

Committing to prepare a detailed forecast at the start of each month was a core foundation of my sales career and completely changed the game for me. Adopting this process and applying it to your investing decisions will likely change the game for you and move you towards becoming a truly sophisticated investor.

The underwriting process you conduct serves as your source of truth and guides your strategic decisions. It is essential that you continuously refer back to the initial forecasts you made during the underwriting stage throughout the project. Some investors make the mistake of neglecting their initial underwriting once the project is underway, which can lead to discrepancies and challenges down the line. Instead, when done well, it serves as the business plan and single source of truth.

Remember that your task is simply to predict what is most likely to happen. And that is likely to be what happened last time. Importantly, this does not mean that you ignore the black swan event or the low-chance, terrible situation or outcome.

No, in fact, underwriting is a process of stress testing many situations. This includes good news, bad news, and all variations in between.

Now that you have the mindset, framework, and tools to underwrite high potential assets, let's talk about how to find the rest of the capital to acquire them.

CHAPTER 15

Cap Tables: The Art of Equity

We now turn our attention back to the capital part of real estate and finding the funds to make great deals happen. Referencing back to our story on the formation of Southwest Airlines, recall that the founder's first thought when considering this business was: "Where would we get the capital?"

In that chapter, I then showed how debt, or borrowed money, can fund the majority of many investment assets you may consider purchasing. Hard physical assets with long useful lives, like airplanes and apartments, are a great fit for debt. That's because if the borrower doesn't pay, then the lender has valuable collateral they can take back, the airplane or the apartment, and sell to get back some or all of the lost loan funds.

So, the use of proper leverage can take care of a big piece of our need for funding. But getting a loan for 100% of the purchase of an income-producing asset is exceedingly rare. Again, the specifics vary widely based on the deal, but a good rule of thumb in commercial real estate is to expect to bring approximately one-third of the purchase price in equity.

Equity shares have a completely different risk and return profile from the capital utilized as debt. But what exactly is equity? Where does it come from? And when you mix funds with other investors, who owns what? What rights does an equity holder have as opposed to a lender?

This chapter will answer these questions and more as we explore the process of raising all the funds to close your deals. In the process, I'll explain some of the specifics of assembling the capital table for a privately funded investment.

Buy Them All

In the months that followed our closing of the DSM2 fund, there were a number of large assets that had come onto the market. While we were in town for an extended summer trip (we wanted to show our commitment to the area, so we rented a house for a few weeks and brought our families out to join us), we toured every property that would let us on-site. We flew home with a ton of momentum and visions of specific deals we had our eyes on.

Two such assets were Court Ave & Marketplace Lofts, and Crosswinds Apartments, both located in central Des Moines. These buildings were 103 and 120 units respectively, and although owned by different groups and being sold for different reasons, both sales were managed by the same broker. We really liked aspects of both deals and decided to make a run at each of them. We underwrote, toured, made initial offers, made the best and final round (where brokers ask a few finalists to submit their sharpest offer), yet were not awarded either of them. Other buyers offered a higher price and we lost out.

Although disappointed, I fully accepted this outcome. We had made a good attempt, but in the end, other buyers were willing to take on more risk to acquire these deals. That's part of honoring a buy box—letting deals go if the price moves past your acceptable range. I remember reviewing the situation with Terrance, who was also disappointed but remained optimistic: "All good, Dan, moving on. And remember, those buyers haven't closed yet; you never know …"

Just a few weeks after saying that, we got wind of another building that was the same size, vintage, and general location as Court Ave & Marketplace Lofts. Riding the positive focus, we dug into the details of this new opportunity known as Harbach Lofts, a beautiful historical restoration right next to major developments downtown. Underwriting and initial tours of this property confirmed that it checked all the boxes for us. We offered a price as high as we were willing to go. However, as the days went by and other offers came in, it was clear we were not going to win this one either. Since that building had a great story and came with some special tax treatment, buyers swarmed the opportunity, and the broker informed us we were actually one of the lowest-priced bids.

Again, we were disappointed as we really liked the building, the location, the story, and the opportunity. But again, we accepted this as part of the game we play and stayed committed to our criteria.

Then, in September, we got wind that the first two deals were having trouble. The other buyers had overextended themselves and were not able to perform on the contracts they had drawn up. Since we had submitted strong offers and had recent history closing transactions with this broker, he called and shared the situation. He also shared the bottom-line number that these now panicked sellers were willing to take. Those numbers were very close to our original bids, so we re-engaged on those opportunities.

Meanwhile, we followed the progress of the Harbach Lofts buyer and saw that there were some delays and challenges brewing for them as well. On another call with Terrance reviewing the evolving situation, I shared, "Man, this is crazy. Amazing assets that we lost out on, and now we might buy them for less than our original number. Which one do you like best?"

My aim with that inquiry was to figure out which deal we'd focus on now that there were options. He was confused by my question as he confirmed that our underwriting said we liked them all. So I clarified my question as I was calculating all the equity that would be needed if all three of these assets ended up back on our plate.

"What will we do if the sellers agree to our terms on all of them?" I asked.

He responded, "Then we buy them all!"

Stay Close to the Rim

The story reinforces the value of "staying close to the rim" regarding deal flow. Sorry for the basketball analogy, but my partners seem to love the sport, and this phrase is commonly used on our calls. And it means, just like a good power forward, we are always looking for a rebound. The reality is, a portion of commercial properties that enter a contract to sell do not close. I was shocked at how common this is when we started, but given that over half of my current portfolio has come through other buyers failing to execute after bidding more than me, I can assure you, it's a valid strategy.

The other lesson derived from this situation would show itself over the following three months as we negotiated, performed due diligence, secured three agency loans, and then raised the necessary equity capital from private investors to fund all of the projects. Yes, as the story continued, we were able to purchase all three buildings due to our being a buyer that provided surety of close. In other words, the sellers felt confident that we could perform after being left at the altar once in this sale process. The ability to do that enabled us to buy them all.

Of course, this "surety of close" is what the market sees, and that's our attitude and conviction when we make an offer and tell a broker they can trust us. However, there is another side of this: the "making of the sausage," if you will. Although we did perform on our contracts and did raise every dollar of equity needed to fully fund all three acquisitions, I can't say it was "easy." In fact, getting all three of these deals to close—which were titled DSM3 and DSM4—became the most difficult thing we'd done since making the move to full-time investment real estate.

Assembling a proper capital table is something I can calmly and easily teach on these pages, and I will do my best to do so here. Like underwriting, there is a bit of science (objectivity) and a bit of art (subjectivity), as I'll explain below. But the real lesson here might be contained in the process to actually make this happen in the timeframe needed in today's environment. Unless you are sitting on piles of personal cash ready to be deployed—assembling and filling a proper capital table might be every investor's biggest hurdle to making an investment happen. Let's review some possible ways to overcome this.

Roles, Risks, and Rewards

Before we get into our options for how to structure and organize those deals, I'll start by stating that anything is possible. If you and a friend or family member have the needed cash to make your dream deal happen, then by all means—keep it simple, stupid (KISS). Do not overcomplicate your structure. Do it yourself without partners if that is possible and if that is clearly what you want and value. If not, add one or two others, and be abundantly clear about roles, risks, and rewards. In that situation, I would hire an attorney to draft proper documents, but you won't need all the details I'm about to share about creating legally compliant investment offerings.

The details below pertain to investments that are large enough to bring in multiple parties that don't have a previous relationship to pool their capital and take a shared risk. The only way to make that happen is to issue a security. Yes, an SEC-regulated investment offering. Because these are so common, the regulating bodies have created some special designations that I'll cover below. This enables you to check all the boxes with the SEC and FINRA but in an expedited manner with the help of specialized attorneys.

First, let's go through some background information on industry standards and legal definitions.

Capital Table

Simply put, a cap table is a detailed list of who owns shares of a company or investment entity. On a basic level, it can be looked at like a pizza, with the size of the slices determined by the percentage of shares. And for basic arrangements, it really can be as simple as that—a list of names and percentages of ownership.

A capital table can also serve a much more sophisticated function and spell out all kinds of nuances in the agreement between the owners. There can be separate classes of equity, priority of payment given to one over the other, custom splits of profit distribution, unequal voting rights, and all kinds of rights of first refusal. These are just a few of the carve-outs that can go into a capital table. Importantly, this document is attached to, or part of, the entity's operating agreement.

Operating Agreement

Everything about how a project and entity will function to the roles of each member is clearly defined in the operating agreement. For example, the capital table will be an exhibit within the operating agreement. This allows the list of equity holders to be kept as a separate document so it can change over time, but the operating agreement can stay the same by simply referring to "Exhibit A."

Importantly, there are no standard or required terms here. There are certainly "market terms" that are commonly found across well-managed agreements, but the details of any agreement between two private parties can be whatever those individuals choose. As I've learned through our projects with Measured Capital, this is not a topic to be penciled in. Due to advice received from mentors and lawyers, Greg and I use this document to clearly define the roles and responsibilities of the managers as well as the limited partners. We also state what would happen in certain situations, how disputes would be resolved, how members could enter or exit the investment, and how the profits of a project will be split, among other necessary declarations. This is best practice and the way you should be looking at an operating agreement, whether you are the one putting it together or signing on as a member.

Classes of Investors

Regardless of what you call it, any large asset like an apartment building needs to be held in a single-purpose LLC. There's a list of reasons for this, your lawyer will be happy to explain. The most common and compliant arrangement to accomplish this is referred to as a "syndication," which is a defined legal structure between the different stakeholders in a project. On a macro level, there are two main classes of shares:

Limited Partners (LP)

Limited partners are the financial partners of a project and will "own" a majority share of any project. Their participation starts and ends with their financial investment. They have full rights of ownership; however, in their limited role, they will generally have no control of the entity or decision-making powers. Along with this comes limitations to their risk—the maximum loss would be the amount of capital they contributed while the maximum gain would be some factor (hopefully a meaningful one) of that original investment.

General Partners (GP)

General partners are the sponsors of the project and serve as its long-term manager.

Accordingly, their share of the capital table will be derived from their work and ability to create investments that generate above-market returns on capital. These individuals (or companies) are listed as the decision-makers in the operating agreements and carry the responsibility to execute the business plan as presented. They have a fiduciary responsibility to the LPs and the capital that funds the project. GPs also carry some form of real risk. They might be required to personally guarantee the loans needed to fund a deal or they could be found of negligence over time and punished in excess of their financial commitment to a project. I don't share that to scare anyone but to set the reality of the GP position and its responsibilities. More on this in the next chapter.

Fees and Promote

The driving motivation for a GP or project sponsor to do the heavy lifting needed to find, acquire, improve, manage, and sell complicated real estate is because there is an opportunity for lucrative profits. That's because GPs usually earn both fees and a share of the profits that they generate for the LPs.

This topic could fill an entire book and that just might be the next topic I publish a full volume on, but for now, let's just use the structure that Measured Capital uses to show how this works. Greg and I have designed it like this to be simple, fair, and create aligned interests.

Fees

For large, syndicated investment projects, there will generally be a few fees charged by the GPs to the funding investment entity. The most common fees are an acquisition fee and asset management fee.

The first is paid after closing the deal. I like to think of this as the "buy-side broker commission." Generally, there is no buy-side broker involved on these assets and, therefore, the cost of sale is only 2% to 3%. The GP often charges a similar fee to reimburse for the cost and effort of deal pursuit. Official due diligence is paid by the investment entity, but at-risk earnest money deposits and steak dinners with the top broker in town are paid for long before an investment entity is formed.

The second is an ongoing fee for managing the asset and executing the plan. Both of these are paid as a form of "salary to the executive team" that are managing these multi-million-dollar assets.

Promote

"Promote" is a fancy term used to describe the profit split that will be calculated as the project produces free cash flow and eventually exits for a capital gain. This will usually be expressed as something like a "70/30 split." That simply means that the profits of an investment will be split with 70% going to the LPs and 30% going to the GPs. It's important to note that only profits above the original investment capital will be split. Whatever money goes in to start is protected as base principal and will be returned at some point in the project cycle. These promote calculations only pertain to net gains.

Cost of Capital

A final lesson before we close this topic—all capital comes with a cost. When I started doing this full time, I had this idea that debt was the scary and risky source of funds and equity was some magical source of funds that barely cost anything. However, from a sponsor standpoint, equity is by far the more expensive of the two and it comes with its own unique obligations. That's because private investors want big returns for taking big leaps of faith in these projects … and they deserve it!

Meanwhile, in the last couple of years, debt has cost sponsors around 3% to 8% annually. Equity in those projects cost 12% to 30%. Yes, equity is more flexible. Equity is more aligned. Equity takes more risk and extends more trust. But equity takes the lion's share of the profits it helps create.

Remember that all capital comes with a cost. The art of assembling a great capital table comes down to determining the right mix of equity and what specific investors are the best fit to participate. There is an argument to be made that nothing will have a bigger impact on the project's success long term than the equity holders and the binding agreement that legally holds title. Get this part right and you'll have a collaborative and patient team supporting the long-term plan.

DSM3 & DSM4

Tying up the loose ends from the story that started this chapter: DSM3 LLC was created to fund the purchase of both Court Ave & Marketplace Lofts and Crosswinds Apartments, and DSM4 LLC was created for Harbach Lofts and the industrial parcel next door. These assets were all acquired well below market value on a "cost-per-door" perspective with each easily satisfying the One Percent Rule.

Following suit with DSM2, we used the same joint venture agreement and simply updated for these particular projects. Measured Capital and VareCo had developed a formulaic approach to splitting the duties and splitting the profits. It allowed each party to do what they do best, staying in their respective zones of genius, while ensuring that together, everyone had everything needed to be successful. Terrance worked the deal terms, Danny got deep into the buildings and plans to execute while Greg and I focused on underwriting and finding the right LPs to fill up the capital table.

DSM3 happened first. We approached our active investors with the opportunity, and all of the available equity was quickly spoken for. The market was dry of good deals, and we had a roster of individuals that understood and agreed with our thesis for Des Moines. The loans took a long time to get approved, but those transactions moved forward basically as expected once we came to the final terms of agreement.

The closing of DSM4 was about two months after the above. It required about the same amount of equity, around $5M, to fund its down payment and required reserves. We had been able to put this amount together twice before in the past year, and honestly it felt like Harbach Loft was the best risk-adjusted deal we had ever done. It was truly an A-class building, and it was certainly the most sophisticated with multiple sources of material income like a retail space, an industrial building, and a Verizon cell phone tower leasing space on-site. It also came with a ten-year business plan and hold period.

Backs Against the Wall

We entered this final capital raise of 2023 with energy and confidence. It was mid-November, and we needed all the funds in one account by December 10 to close. If it didn't, we opened ourselves up to a repricing of the loan, forfeiture of deposits, and possibly even losing the buildings altogether. These were all very risky and expensive potential paths.

However, the buildings showed so well and the investment forecast so solid, we figured there would be a line out the door. Instead, we filled about two-thirds of the required investment and then fell flat. It was the week of Thanksgiving and not a great time to be bothering busy people about funding a real estate deal. The few contacts that had expressed interest were not answering the phone, so we started to feel a bit trapped. The deficit was over $1M and loomed over us for nearly two weeks as we approached the closing date.

I'm happy to say that we "figured it out"—much like Greg predicted in this book's Introduction story. Parkinson's Law states that "work gets done in the time we give it." Our backs were up against the wall, and creative solutions began to present themselves. The details of this rollercoaster will be saved for another time, but no doubt it was a transformative experience for me and Greg as investment sponsors. As he commented right after we had secured the last dollar, "Man, this business is not for the faint of heart."

We learned so many lessons about what we did wrong here. From the timing of our message to the communication mediums we chose to our attitude and assumptions going in. Bringing in some of our original frameworks—I didn't say this road would be easy, but I did think it would be worth it. Some deals have come together like a small jigsaw puzzle with all the pieces nicely arranged. Other deals have a bunch of puzzle pieces missing, and it's our job to figure out how to make the whole thing work or be smart enough to move on and pass when it's just not meant to be.

Cap Tables Matter

No matter how you slice it, a capital table full of equity is absolutely necessary to be successful in this game. And that cash must be aligned, patient, and high trust. Without this, it's going to be very hard to be successful in the private investing game.

Importantly, this topic is usually a fork in the road for investors. They are either interested in putting deals together by raising capital from outsiders and then managing that capital or they are not. From firsthand experience, I can share that it's an intense responsibility and not one to be taken lightly.

On the other hand, many investors decide that they are more comfortable and a better fit to play the LP and participate in these deals but not turn it into a business by taking outside investment. And as mentioned above, there is no specific way these capital tables must be structured. They can be simple and include nobody but yourself or a family member. They can be large syndicated entities with a number of investors with various backgrounds, beliefs, expectations, and desires. There are many paths to accomplish this, but there is no doubt that having "dry powder" readily available as an investment sponsor is a major competitive advantage. As our examples in this chapter showed, when capital is well organized and ready to go, it can help "buy them all."

Moving to the next chapter, we take this discussion deeper and look at the highly-misunderstood concept of control, which is very different from equity ownership.

CHAPTER 16

Passive, Active, or In Control?

A common error of beginning investors is thinking they must have total control over their investments. It's natural to want control and to think that will be best. It's also common to think that having control will reduce the risk of an investment. As high achievers, many individuals that make the move to private investing are used to being in charge and in control. They have high expectations of themselves and love to take on responsibility.

But isn't that how the High Achievement Trap gets set to begin with? Through the illusion of control? It's exactly here, when taking on something new, that we overestimate our abilities, our time, and our capacity, that stress builds up and we earn that sense of overwhelm. And that is the opposite of what we are going for here.

While not advocating for blindly giving up control, I will make a strong argument in this chapter that it is not always better or less risky to be in a controlling position. In fact, private equity investing might just be your best chance to practice giving up control.

Give It Up?

The first reason I encourage this is that control comes with the responsibility of decision-making. By this, I mean that the controlling member of any investment must make the decisions necessary to maintain profitable financial statements. Yes, it can be a privilege to have decision-making powers, but only when someone is confident in the decisions that they will face. Otherwise, it becomes an obligation.

Along with this is the consideration of being properly educated, qualified, and interested in making certain decisions. I can share from firsthand experience that controlling the operations of commercial real estate isn't always pleasant. It can be messy on the inside. There are evictions and insurance claims and tax bills and attorneys (lots of attorneys). There can be competitive pressures and poor collections and overwhelming mortgage payments.

Again, the whole point of this book is to prepare you to create investments that minimize the chances of such problems coming up, but realistically speaking, these issues could present themselves at any given property. Great controlling operators with the skills, resources, and bandwidth to manage assets can and will overcome these issues. But then consider the busy executive with a big time corporate job who is doing real estate as a side hustle. They are unlikely to make the same strategic decisions or skillfully navigate a challenging period.

The reality is that a $20M apartment building is a $20M business, and it deserves a qualified and active management team just like any business with that valuation.

The question we'll be answering here is whether you want or need to be a part of that management team in order to achieve your investing goals.

Passive Investor, Passive Income

The real reason behind this chapter is the world's obsession with passive income. And, for that matter, my obsession with passive income. When it comes to money, what could be better than fresh cash showing up in your bank account each month without any effort or hassle placed upon you to receive it?

As someone who searched for nearly a decade before finding my first sustainable source of passive income, I'm well versed with its pitfalls. The crucial point to grasp is this: generating truly passive income requires passive ownership, meaning limited ownership where the decision-making authority lies with someone else, not you.

Otherwise, it's not passive. If you are directly responsible for the outcomes of the investment, then there is some active element, and you've got work to do. I've learned this lesson owning a bunch of single-family rental homes, and I've learned it owning small businesses. When I compare those experiences with owning shares of stock in a public company—the difference is stark. The public company stock is completely passive. If I showed up at the Apple corporate headquarters and demanded some respect as an "owner" of the company, they'd call security. I own 0.00000001% of the company, and my shares come with language that clearly states my opinion about the operations of the company do not matter. In other words, I have zero control on the financial performance of Apple stock.

Now take the rental homes and the small businesses I've owned. I'm the CEO, the CFO, the chairman of the board, and everything else that doesn't fall on a hired employee or vendor. And who hires those employees and vendors? I do. Because I'm the owner.

Folks, this is not passive.

Some small business owners are able to get themselves out of the day-to-day and install a general manager or even an executive suite full of managers if the company is large enough. I'll recognize here that the income generated from this will likely qualify as passive for tax treatment by the IRS, and I agree it's semi-passive in character. But again, if you retain control at a board level and can fire the executive team at your leisure, is it really passive ownership?

I make this point in depth because it underpins the thesis of this chapter—that having absolute control might not always be the best thing. This choice will be unique to each investor. First, let's think about what gives an investment the best chances of success.

Who's the Most Qualified?

During my first projects as a deal sponsor, I held a number of Zoom calls with potential investors to review the properties Measure Capital was buying. As mentioned, many of my early deals were completed as partnerships with proven sponsors, so I brought along the other GPs to assist me in fielding questions on these calls. I remember one moment so clearly.

There was a potential LP, who was clearly anxious about the decision, that shared he was on the fence and that he couldn't get over the idea of giving up control for this large of a capital investment. I'll never forget the response to his concern: "Well, I'll explain it like this: who do you want making the decisions about this asset long term, the guy that found it, improved it, managed it, and does that same thing to lots of other buildings and has been for years … or the guy that lives a thousand miles away, has never been to the property, and focuses on something else all day?"

It was a high-trust call and the message was well received. That investor agreed to move forward with us. This experience totally changed my perspective because up until that point, I insisted on having a controlling stake in any private investments.

Control vs. Rights

A very important qualifier here: I'm referring to operating control and the responsibility to manage an asset throughout its life. However, giving up control does not mean giving up your rights. The operating agreement that is established to hold the property will contain immense detail of the rights and responsibilities of each party—specifically the LP and the GP.

In a fair agreement, LPs retain rights to exert influence or assume control if a project isn't going according to plan. LPs also have capacities to inspect the property, the entity's financial statements, and other rights that outsiders do not have. Finally, standard US contract and securities law provide LPs with certain minimum rights, regardless of the agreement.

In addition to these standard rights, there can be custom language added to any agreement to bring more power to the LPs, even while ceding operating control to another party. This would include the decision of when to sell the building, when to admit new members to the capital table, or when to refinance the primary mortgage. Each of these are material events that can be called out specifically, and the power can be granted to a different party or shared amongst multiple parties. Implementing these safeguards is beyond the scope here, but an attorney can help you understand how to "write in" certain powers to a partnership or joint venture agreement. Just make sure, if you dip into decision-making authority, that these are rights you really need and are qualified to hold.

Potential Roles

In the last chapter, we reviewed the legal structure and defined roles in a syndicated private equity investment— namely the LP and the GP. Below, we'll look at these roles again, but from a more practical—rather than a legal—view. I see three paths that any investor can pursue as it relates to their role in commercial real estate investments. Those three choices are (1) passive, (2) active, or (3) in control.

1—Passive

This first level is for the LP. Their ownership is passive because these individuals have no operating authority. They are generally along for the ride. This is the preferred path, so the investor can get back to their normal job, business, or whatever they do with their time that the increased passive income can now support.

2—Active

The next step up is reserved for a GP who is not in direct control of all decisions related to the investment but is part of the management team and has influence. I have this position in a number of deals and believe it works very well for all the reasons described above.

Again, this "active but non-controlling" GP is really only going to occur in large deals with big capital requirements. But in those situations, it often takes more than one talented GP to ensure a successful deal, and somebody needs to have the final say.

3—In Control

Finally, there is the one party that is legally "in control." This can be an individual, or it can be a business. There is no official title for this role; however, "lead sponsor" and "managing member" could both qualify. They carry the duty and responsibility to look after the investment and keep it compliant with all local laws, the lender's requirements, the taxing authorities, and the city inspector. They also must keep it staffed with a capable property management team and ensure it's marketable to future renters and the business plan is executed so the property can be sold for a profit long term.

For this responsibility, the controlling party will be rewarded with the bulk of fees and promote profits that are generated from the investment. And well deserved!

An important note here: any cash that a controlling sponsor contributes to a deal's capital table should be classified as LP shares and treated the same as all other LP-contributed capital. There is a common pool of equity, often referred to as "A shares" in the legal agreement that all carry the same rights and terms.

Creating Alignment

A theme throughout this book has been to encourage more alignment in your investing. I firmly believe there is no objective "better" in life. The idea of something being "better" comes down to unique individual perspectives and definitions of success. So let's refer back to Chapter 2 where I helped you define your own definition of success and create a vision that inspires you. What were your core answers to that exercise?

Was it the financial rewards? Increasing freedom of time and location? Accelerating your timeframe to retirement?

Or was it about learning the skills needed to become a world-class investor? Building relationships and trust with influential people that can help scale your portfolio?

Both of these are valid answers and lines of thinking. But each shows a different primary interest and would encourage different paths.

The first set of answers is perfect for the non-controlling investor. In this case, a big focus should be finding and selecting high-quality sponsors that originate deals within a buy box you believe in. The second set of answers is more aligned with how I was thinking when I sold my business and entered professional free agency. Accordingly, that sent me down a very active path where I delayed my expectations for financial returns but planted seeds for a new professional focus and life experience. That's what I was looking for and focused on.

Perceived vs. Actual Control

A final point before we wrap up—high achievers love control. More specifically, they love to feel in control. This is often driven by the belief that our individual success is due to our ability to control our situation and drive positive outcomes. There may be some truth to that, and you may have examples of this in your own life, but let's step back a minute and think about our relationship to control and exactly what it gets us.

Let's use an example on a large scale to highlight. Is Jeff Bezos in total control of Amazon? Well, legally speaking, he is the highest authority and top decision-maker. So as a stockholder, you're relinquishing your control to him. At the same time, is he really making decisions about how the customer service agents are responding to inquiries in the chat box? Or the pricing strategy for its massive toy sales promotion during the holidays? Or who they will promote to be manager of the distribution facilities for western states? No, no, and absolutely not. There are millions of decisions that take place every day inside the walls of Amazon that he is not privy to. Nowadays, the organizational structure and operating systems and corporate governance policies do most of the controlling.

However, if this was different, and Amazon didn't have all those management systems and controls in place, and Bezos really did control every detail, the company would be a disaster. He couldn't possibly make all the decisions needed to enable the company to run effectively. Other high-performing executives would resign if they lost the slices of control they currently hold. And our control freak Bezos wouldn't get any sleep because of the non-stop flow of big decisions he'd need to make just to stay online. He'd have zero bandwidth for strategy or exit planning or talking to investment bankers about recapitalizing the company's ever-expanding wealth.

As ridiculous as that example might sound, it has happened before and on a much larger scale—the Communist party that ruled over the USSR during much of the 20th century. That was a centralized government where all the control and decision-making authority was held by a small group of men located in one capital city. The experiment lasted nearly 70 years, and although it looked okay on the surface for a few decades, this obsession with central control eventually produced more poverty, starvation, and human atrocities than any other governing body in human history. It's a real-life example of the that-would-never-happen situation with Bezos above, and it went down about as poorly as possible.

The ability to accept some chaos is a needed trait to play big in real estate and private investing. It's a dynamic ride if you insist on living the ups and downs of each day. Instead, my best practice is to give up control on many small details while having influence and veto power that can be used in important situations. I'm playing the long game and have adjusted my "control dial" down quite a bit.

Remember, I love control as much as anybody. Making this shift internally has been one of the most challenging tasks along this journey. But my goal is abundance and freedom. Having the responsibility to control all the decisions across hundreds of apartment doors would not provide me the freedoms that I'm going for.

The Right Mix

Concluding this analysis of control—the right answer will be specific to each investor and will land somewhere on this broad scale. Too much will stress you out because you'll be more active and have more demands than desired. Too little will stress you out because you'll feel "out of control" and exposed with your investment capital. Finding that right mix is my definition of success.

Remember that truly passive income will require a truly passive ownership position and mindset. Importantly, this does not have to come with any less legal protection or rights. In fact, with proper legal support, we can define just the right amount of influence and protection.

Because just as we need to take a hard look at our relationship to control as we move forward in our investment journey, we will also benefit from faith in our vision and discipline to stay with it.

CHAPTER 17

Unwavering Faith and Long-Term Discipline

Back at the start of 2022 when this whole "lock up a 100-unit deal" thing began and I made the internal commitment to make it happen, I fully believed "it" would occur in Jacksonville, Florida. I have history there, I have family living there, and I've even directly owned rental real estate there. Surely, I thought, my entry back into real estate as a business would start here.

Accordingly, visiting Jacksonville was the first thing I did when I started taking action. I found every broker in town, scheduled a coffee meeting with half of them, and got on a plane to see what kind of apartments I could buy. I explored much of north and central Florida for potential. Much like the first time I got on a plane to check out Florida real estate over ten years prior, I was a bit surprised by what I found. But rather than real estate being *on fire* sale, it was straight up on fire. There was a buying frenzy. When I started getting potential properties sent my way, they would be under contract with another buyer faster than I could finish my initial review. And they were going for prices that my financial models just couldn't support.

I kept communication going with all the active brokers to stay in the mix, but the feedback made my head shake. Value-add deals, which means older vintage and needing work, were selling for less than a 4% cap rate. (That's extremely low and calculates to crazy high valuations.) Buyers were using high-risk and high-leverage bridge loans to fund just about every deal that closed. Multiple offers and hard money deposits were common in order to lock up any asset coming to market.

It was all very discouraging.

During this period, I attended a number of conferences and seminars dedicated to multifamily investing, and one such event focused on underwriting and forecasting. In preparation of the event, the speaker asked for example deals and questions related to them. I took the opportunity and sent in a deal I had recently lost out on in Jacksonville and posed the question: "How does someone pay 30% higher than what I came up with?"

This question and deal got the presenter's attention, so the next morning turned into an hour-long session with over a hundred people all looking at the details of this deal. We checked all the assumptions and the audience asked questions.

After going through it in depth, the conclusion of the instructor, and the whole room for that matter was—"We don't see it either." His advice was to stick to my buy box. The model says it's overvalued, so it's overvalued for me, and I shouldn't buy it. Wait for the next one.

So I waited. And I underwrote new deals. And I got outbid.

Over and over. This went on for nearly two years.

Unwavering Faith

Meanwhile, as the frustration increased regarding deal flow in Florida, Greg and I purchased a quick 800 units between Waco and Des Moines, all of which hit our required metrics and more. I didn't give up on my hometown, but doubt did begin to creep in. As it happened, on the last day of the same conference above, I was in the audience when they welcomed Hal Elrod to the stage for the closing keynote speech. Hal is the author of the book *The Miracle Equation*, his second best-selling book that teaches achieving any major goal or "miracle" requires we adopt the mantra:

> *"I am committed to maintaining unwavering faith that I will reach my goal and putting forth extraordinary effort until I do, no matter what."*

This message hit me at the perfect time. I was fresh off the public underwriting session and a room full of peers and experts agreeing with my perspective. So I wrote this phrase down on the notepad I had with me at the time and decided this was how it would happen. With unwavering faith and extraordinary effort. I decided right there that my vision would come to be, but I would not force it. I refused to give it a deadline; even if it took years and a full market reset, I had unwavering faith it would be realized.

Discipline Equals Freedom

Making the proclamation that "I have faith" and actually acting on that faith over a long and challenging journey requires something else: discipline.

I had a challenging relationship with discipline for most of my life. I saw it as constrictive and overbearing. I tried to avoid discipline because I saw it as opposing the freedoms that I value so much. All of that changed when I came across another impactful quote. This time, it was from the ancient Greek philosopher Aristotle:

"Through discipline comes freedom."

At the time, I was at a low point in my entrepreneurial journey and looking for answers internally. I had read a number of books on Stoicism and was attempting to adopt more of that mindset into my daily thinking. Epictetus and Marcus Aurelius, who emphasized the importance of self-control and personal responsibility in achieving a fulfilling life, were constantly in the back of my mind, reminding me to chill out and accept my reality, whatever that might be. However, I was really just using discipline to get more stuff done. I wasn't aligned with it helping my level of freedom.

As I continued to read, I learned that high performers in every field adopt this attitude. It was actually a story about the lives and careers of two of the greatest basketball players of all time, Kobe Bryant and LeBron James, that brought this home for me. These two guys have been at the absolute pinnacle of their profession. Successful, wealthy, and famous beyond measure. They could "go anywhere and do anything" as a result of their accomplishments.

But the punchline is that these are also two of the most disciplined athletes of all time. Part of Kobe's lore is his relentless training schedule and dedication to practice. Former teammates tell stories of his marathon shooting sessions. After a normal NBA practice, he would remain at the gym for hours, shooting three-pointers and free-throws until he was satisfied with his performance. LeBron is known for a similar approach—early morning training followed by strict diet and recovery regimens. His commitment to maintaining peak physical condition has allowed him to remain one of the top players in the NBA well into his late thirties.

These attitudes and work ethics set a standard for the teams these two have played on and raised the bar of the whole squad. As a result, they've brought home more championship rings. And what happens when you are disciplined enough to win at the highest level with a game you love to play? You get rewarded with lots of freedom.

JAX1

In 2023, my personal equivalent of winning the NBA Finals was purchasing a deal in Jacksonville that fit my buy box. It took extreme patience, but finally, over two years after starting the search, we signed the deed for a 64-unit asset that made great financial sense and was a perfect fit for our thesis.

Closing this deal was far from a straight path, and it tested both my faith and my discipline. But in hindsight, it was also a culmination of everything we've talked about in the past ten or so chapters. Greg and I were clear in our thesis and communicated it to everyone we worked with. Some snickered or even laughed, saying our requirements were too conservative to ever win deals in Jacksonville's competitive environment. But we stayed with it and proved to everyone that these deals existed somewhere, and we were a sure thing as a buyer if an asset hit those metrics.

When the broker first called about Hidden Oaks, his story included two failed attempts to close on the property in the prior year. That put the owner in a bad mood but also accepting of a new price that likely wasn't on the table for the first set of buyers.

This was our moment. Greg and I made the offer that we were told would get it done. Our terms were accepted, and we started due diligence. The equity for the deal came together quickly as a number of our major investors were excited for the first taste of Jacksonville. Things were running smoothly until we hit some major hurdles with the loan application and approval process.

The ups and downs of this are too nuanced to go through here, but I can summarize to say that we were forced to run parallel loan applications at a local bank and with an agency lender for over 60 days before getting the final approval needed to close. And that approval came just 24 hours before the term of our purchase contract expired. One more full business day of delays and the seller could have walked off with $150,000 of earnest money deposits, and we'd be the third party to fail at closing this deal. Instead, all funds transferred at exactly the right time, and we've been happy owners since.

As Mr. Elrod encouraged at the start of this chapter, sometimes getting a big private investment deal closed requires "unwavering faith and extraordinary effort." Bring this attitude to your deals and decisions, and I believe you'll bring chance on your side.

Structured Success

As we close this topic out, I'll invite Marcus Aurelius back into the conversation. He once said, "You have power over your mind—not outside events. Realize this, and you will find strength."

These words encapsulate the essence of discipline. In the context of investing, it means that while we cannot control market fluctuations, economic cycles, or external circumstances, we can control our responses, our strategies, and our commitment to our goals. Sometimes, the results come quickly and seem almost to be easy. Other times, the journey to our goals is long, arduous, and makes us question our sanity. Leaning on the tools and resources from earlier chapters sets us up to be able to do this once we are deep into that journey.

For JAX1 and the long-term belief in a city with strong fundamentals and big upside, we're finally in the game because we stayed committed with "unwavering faith" to making it happen. Speaking of getting in the game …

CHAPTER 18

Get in the Game

In the final months of my career as a technology sales person working for commissions, I was spending a lot of my time after work each night dreaming up new businesses and researching investment ideas. I was desperate to find a new professional path.

Looking back, I realize this was the first time I found myself in a High Achievement Trap.

One of the resources that landed in my inbox during that time of discovery was the book titled *The Lean Startup* by Eric Ries. This work came out in 2011 and at the time, the ideas were cutting edge. Ries explains early in the book that his method "favors experimentation over elaborate planning, customer feedback over intuition, and iterative design over traditional up front development." He emphasizes that the true measure of progress for a startup or innovative project is not the amount of effort or resources expended, but rather the validated learning and improvement that is generated.

The key principle that underpins this methodology is the concept of the minimum viable product (MVP). The MVP is a rudimentary version of the product or service that captures its core functionality and value proposition, and is released to some "beta" or test users as quickly as possible. Once released, feedback is gathered and the product is iterated to improve based on what these active customers are saying. This process is then repeated and over time, the original MVP evolves into a full-blown suite of products that serves its core customer.

This process is so effective, it is now considered standard best practice in the world of software startups and downright archaic to do it any other way. Prior to this idea, entrepreneurs would go into "stealth mode" and try to create a perfect product in isolation, but it rarely worked. Through the MVP process, many of the biggest brands in technology today started with embarrassingly simple products. Let's highlight three great examples.

AirBnB's first version rented out an air mattress in an apartment during a busy conference in San Francisco. The founders had some extra space and knew the local hotels were sold out. Someone bought their offer and the delivery worked. So they did it again. This software is now worth approximately $100B and rents millions of homes, rooms, and beds every month.

Salesforce.com's original product was a very simple online version of a customer database. Its founder, Marc Benioff, was an executive at Oracle and was frustrated with the extremely high entry price for decent customer resource management (CRM) software, so he slapped together a bare-bones application that stored contact information and opportunities for salespeople. By targeting small businesses and entrepreneurs, he actually used its simplicity as its main selling point. As the customer base grew, so did the demands for new features—pushing the company to expand into every corner of cloud-based business software and $25B in annual recurring revenues.

Okay, one more example.

Amazon's original service was selling books online. The only products on their virtual shelves for the first five years were books. That was it, and no one really expected them to do anything else. And it was a rough ride proving that a company could effectively market and sell products online, process payments, ship packages, handle returns, and all the rest that goes into e-commerce at scale. None of that existed at the time.

Bezos's MVP was nothing more than "online book store." However, he understood that if he could get books to work, he could likely sell anything online. So in the sixth year, they added CDs and computer games. In the seventh year, they opened up the marketplace concept, and their catalog quickly swelled to millions of products from every category under the sun. Building out a logistics empire to support deliveries became a natural byproduct of this, as did AWS, the concept of renting out the extra capacity on their network of web servers to other companies. Both of those are now multi-billion-dollar business units.

Each of these examples reminds us of the power of focusing on creating some kind of beginning, no matter how small. The magic lies in getting started and out of the blocks. The opposite of this is what is popularly referred to as "paralysis by analysis." We'll get to that in a moment. First, let's connect Benioff and Bezos' rise to your own plans for becoming a world-class investor.

Minimum Viable Investment

While Ries and *The Lean Startup* are credited with popularizing the idea of MVP, I'd like to introduce my own twist on that framework—minimum viable investment (MVI).

MVI replicates the process and the rationale of MVP, but applies the theory to the journey of the individual investor looking to play on a bigger stage. Although your long-term goal might be to own hundreds of units or whatever floats your boat—the reality is you are not going to start there. If you don't yet own an apartment building, or some other cash-flowing commercial real estate or small business asset, then I propose that the most important next step for you is to own a slice of such a deal. And to do so with some level of urgency.

I'm not suggesting you run out and buy the next building you tour or commit to the next syndicated offering to hit your inbox—but if you are acting on the steps presented above, at this point in your journey and in this book, you are fully prepared to create a simple thesis based on your opinion, find a partner or sponsor to work with, and start.

Meanwhile, although I'm all about minimizing the equity component of deals and making really efficient use of the cash you deploy, I also recognize that you aren't really investing until you are contributing your own cash to the equity stack of the deal. The awesome annualized returns and cash dividends available through apartment investing applies to the equity that is actively invested. The more cash you put into a deal like that, the more that comes out.

So on that topic—start small, but start meaningful. Decide what is the minimum cash contribution you are willing to make to earn a meaningful stake in a privately held asset. It might be $50k, $100k, or $500k. It's all relative to our individual situations.

Defining your minimum viable investment is work that can be done in the next 30 days. This book has already laid out the process to follow. By modifying your goal and focusing on the minimum to "get in the game," then I believe you can massively accelerate your entrance to the game and to scaling within the game.

Additionally, if you like what you've heard about Measured Capital, our thesis and competitive advantage, there could be an opportunity to invest with us.

Get In Touch

If the ideas in this book speak to you, we'd love to connect and see if Measured Capital's upcoming investment opportunities could be a fit to help you accomplish your unique goals. We are able to onboard a limited number of new investors each quarter. To start the process, please visit us at the link below, and fill out the form to see if we'd be a good fit for one another:

measuredcapital.invportal.com/signup

Learn and Iterate

Any investor that currently sits atop a profitable real estate portfolio has likely been on a challenging journey creating it. Through all the mistakes, market volatility, and the slow grind up and to the right—all veteran investors got there by dealing with challenges the best they can and learning along the way.

Seth Godin, the renowned marketer and author who pens a daily newsletter to millions around the globe, has a famous phrase that supports the ideas driving this chapter: "shipped is better than perfect." With these words, he is denouncing perfection while extolling the power the progress. It encourages us to embrace a mindset of action, iteration, and continuous improvement, rather than getting stuck in endless cycles of polishing and refinement.

Perfection is the enemy of progress, and this hesitation petrifies many people and keeps them on the sidelines. They never do deals. They don't know how to process risk and accept that some things are simply out of their control.

The reality is, your first deal won't be perfect. Yes, it will likely have plenty of risks associated with it. And yes, you will make mistakes. The results could even be worse than expected!

And I present to you—this is a good thing. If your first deal was your best deal, then what would that say about the rest of your investing career? I'm aiming to improve my skills, deal flow, capital structure, and leverage on every single new project.

Let's come back to reality and realize that one good investment will not secure your long-term fortune. More than likely, to create significant wealth, an investor needs to stay with it for decades and purchase a series of high-quality assets, sell, or refinance a few times, and experience the compounding effect of appreciation at scale.

Again, as I've preached throughout these pages, you, as an individual investor, can massively reduce the risk of the investments you are involved in. By having a clear thesis, developing a competitive advantage, sticking to a buy box, and partnering with high-quality people that leverage your strengths—you too can become a successful private investor.

APPENDIX

Appendix A

Advanced Return Metrics

Below are terms that I use nearly every day when I'm engaged in the art of creating and managing private investments.

Capitalization Rate: Cap Rate

(Net Operating Income / Asset Price)

Commonly referred to as the "cap rate," you'll see this metric used to measure the price and potential return of a real estate asset. The formula computes the yield of a property over a one-year time horizon assuming the property is purchased all cash and not with a loan.

One analogy I use with many investors that seems to stick is that of a business multiple. Just as an operating business is valued as a multiple of its earnings or revenue, so is income-producing real estate; but it's expressed in reverse. A multiple is, well, multiplied into a figure to get the value. Cap rates, rather, are the result of dividing income into the price and are expressed as a percentage. This number will then tell you how much annualized income you can expect to receive given the price paid.

Because it is used so commonly, it is hands down the most misunderstood and misapplied metric in the business. The first and most important rule I'd like to impart here—higher cap rates are not objectively better. This is because cap rates are only useful in a relative sense. Although higher rates means higher income and returns on capital, there is much more to consider here.

Let's use a simple example to illustrate: asset A is a brand-new, 300-unit apartment tower in the hottest part of town packed full of young professionals. Asset B is a run-down 90-unit building just outside the suburbs with working class renters and monthly evictions. Asset A would likely trade around a 3% to 4% cap rate while Asset B would trade for a 6% to 8% cap rate.

So which asset is better? Which would you rather own? The one that looks really nice or the one that makes the most money? The one that is easy to keep full of great tenants but barely clears its debt payment? Or the one that has constant turnover but produces huge cash flow at the end of each month?

This example also points to the second major use of cap rates: they also serve as a measurement of risk. Yes, from a market perspective—higher returns come with higher risks. Asset A from our example is unlikely to have any maintenance issues or leasing challenges for years while it reigns as the nicest building in town. Low risk, low cap rates.

Regarding these low cap rate assets, they can be very challenging on the acquisition side because once they get low enough (around 3.5%), the cash flow of a project disappears. However—when you turn around to sell that asset, you will simply love low cap rates because that is what drives the price of the asset so high in certain appreciation-heavy markets.

A final point on cap rates. They are used in the context of acquisition to measure cost of the income (in-place cap rate), they are used in the context of a sale to capture unrealized gains (terminal cap rate), and they are used while holding an asset to express the state of operations (stabilized cap rate). There is also the concept of "market cap rates" that move over time along with local and national trends. Each of these is a very specific measure at a specific point in time. What I've learned is that many people mistake the particular version of the "cap rate" they are referring to and apply it to the wrong situation. Therefore, when utilizing cap rates in your analysis, be very specific about which type of cap rate you are referring to.

Average Rate of Return: ARR

(Average Annual Return / Initial Investment)

This is as simple as it gets for understanding returns, as everyone seems to be able to grasp the concept of "average." If we have a deal that generates 6% in year one, and 10% in year two, then we have an investment with an 8% ARR.

Amazingly, although I find this to be a totally incomplete measure of financial performance, it's also the only metric used by the financial industry to market mutual funds and publicly regulated investments. This is the percentage that will be printed next to the ticker symbol in a financial advisor's prospectus. Because the industry and its SEC regulator's job is to protect investors, they have a mandate to simplify and not confuse.

The problem is that with this measure alone, I have no idea when I'm getting the profits or what needs to happen to get them. However, since it is so prevalent and simple, it's a number we need to understand and put in its proper place.

Internal Rate of Return: IRR

((Future Value / Present Value) ^ (1 / Number of Periods) – 1)

Yup, that's the formula. That's actually a highly simplified version of the formula that reduces multiple other necessary calculations. The good news is that you don't need to memorize this formula. Honestly, no one does outside developers that create financial modeling software. We have access to many Excel templates that can produce this number with a couple of inputs. The important part is understanding what it means and why it's different.

The easiest way to think about IRR is realizing that it's not much different from something you already know. IRR is just average returns (ARR) with consideration for when the actual payments occur. Rather than treating all profits as if they were the same, IRR weighs the income you get based on when you get it.

A quick example: if you buy an asset with $1M of equity and 5 years later sell it and get back $2M of equity, that's a great return. The $1M of profit over 5 years would come out to $200k per year, which is a nice and clean 20% average return, or ARR. However, when looking at this deal from an IRR perspective, the deal is generating ~15% internal rate of return. That gap is because the investor had to wait 5 years to get back a single dollar. And in investing, time is money.

Now if we take that exact same deal, but instead of waiting until the end to get the $1M gain, you actually received that profit evenly, with $200k of cash coming back to you each year from operations. At the end of the project, you'd again have a 20% average returns, but the IRR would also equal 20% since the timing of the cash flow was in perfect alignment with the calendar. For the record, this almost never happens in actual investing; cash flows will vary month to month and quarter to quarter.

At the end of the day, IRR reigns supreme with highly sophisticated investors. IRR emphasizes that sooner is better when it comes to receiving returns and it is the deciding judge between two otherwise equal investments for institutions and investment committees. It's also taught in every business valuation class in the world, so the infatuation with IRR might just be a bunch of MBAs flexing the formulas they were forced to learn in graduate school!

Cash-on-Cash Return: CoC

(Annual Cash Flow / Cash Invested)

This is the formula that I started with 15 years ago before pulling the trigger on my first investment property, and it's still my favorite today. Although I must calculate IRR and other metrics to consider the efficiency of capital and to compare alternative strategies, nothing speaks to me as an individual investor like cash-on-cash returns. It even sounds cool, right? Because what's better than cash? Cash on cash!

Simply put, it's the amount of cash I receive each year divided by the cash I originally put in. If I invest $100,000, and each year I get back $20,000 in cash from the profits of holding the assets, then I have 20% cash-on-cash returns.

The reason CoC is so important to me is because I plan to (soon) live entirely on cash flow returns. As a sponsor organizing deals with other investors, I also put a ton of value on CoC because it provides margin for error. As I learned to scale up my investments to the hundreds-of-units-per-deal range, I also learned that big CoC returns are rare. Large assets, especially those with value-add business plans, often have to be sold to unlock the value created while the owner held and improved it. This idea of waiting until an exit event to realize my profits is challenging. I've sold real estate and businesses before, and nothing is guaranteed until the escrow check clears. So although many deals look to be winners when projecting a future sale price, at Measured Capital, Greg and I prefer assets that pay us every month. And if for some reason we are off in our assumptions and the business plan goes awry, I have all that potential cash-on-cash return to burn off before the asset truly becomes a problem to hold long term.

If you purchase a deal and expect to have zero cash flow, then things go wrong, that means negative cash flow and the clock starts ticking much louder. As mentioned before, it just doesn't make a ton of sense to me to buy real estate, separate with a bunch of cash, and not receive any ongoing reward. Of course, I've witnessed deals where investors double and triple their money in less than a year. These deals happen all the time and are the strategic counter to my demand for cash-on-cash returns.

An important clarifier that comes up in almost every conversation about cash-on-cash: yes, this metric considers the effect of loans and leverage. The very first metric, capitalization rate, is the popular measure that strips out the impact of financing, but not cash-on-cash. This is the metric that looks at post-debt cash flow to see exactly how much return your original capital is generating from the regular operations of the asset.

Yield on Cost: YOC

(Net Operating Income / Total Cost)

When I started to submit multifamily deals to banks for terms sheets and preapprovals, I began to see this yield-on-cost term get thrown around a lot more. Then I started hanging out with some big players in the commercial mortgage industry and realized this is the preferred metric to evaluate the total risk of a project and how efficient you are with the capital being deployed.

The big difference between this formula and the others that we've considered is that term "cost." When acquiring commercial real estate, it's rare for the new investor to fail to bring some kind of capital improvement budget. This is needed to perform upfront improvements, address deferred maintenance, and set the asset up for leasing success. It's also necessary to add that budget to the purchase price to get the total cost and consider the true operating yield. So, in this formula, we add that CapEx budget (and all other fees and costs related to securing the deal) to the price paid to arrive at total cost.

Banks and the finance type love this because it's big picture and they can apply it to different moments in time to compare the change and trends. Often, experienced investors want to see something like "a 2% increase in yield on cost between purchase and year three." That would mean the deal has stabilized and is producing their desired level of income.

Multiple on Invested Capital: MOIC

(Total Cash Inflows / Total Cash Outflows)

This measure is expressed as a number like "2.16x," and it works exactly as it sounds, i.e., a multiple on invested capital. We simply multiply the MOIC value by the original investment amount. That would mean if you put in $100,000, you'd get back $216,000 over the life of the investment. The obvious problem is there is no respect for timeframe. An MOIC of 2.16x is great over five years, but if it took 15 to 20 years, I'd find other places for my capital.

This one was totally new to me when I started reviewing the pitch decks and investment analysis of other sponsors doing private equity deals. This is a very common metric in retail private equity pitch decks. I assume this is because of its simplicity. An expected MOIC combined with expected hold period is a very straight path to understanding total return.

Appendix B
Advanced Lending Terms & Metrics

Appendix B offers a review of the most important commercial real estate loan terms and metrics.

Loan Types

Before we get into evaluating a loan, let's understand the few key types of loans as each has its own range of terms and reasons to use.

Agency

This is a term used to describe loans issued by Fannie Mae and Freddie Mac's multifamily divisions. These are where government policy and credit insurance come into play for investment assets. The terms of these loans are almost always the best although the underwriting is strict and the process is cumbersome. Regulation is the root cause of both of those outcomes. Greg and I love agency loans because we get years of benefit after 60 days of pain. Additionally, they carry a feature that truly sets them apart for investors looking to acquire vast portfolios involving hundreds of millions of dollars—these are "non-recourse" loans, which means the lender can't come after personal assets if the borrower defaulted on the loan for some reason. Personal guarantees are going to be required for most forms of lending outside of this and the next categories.

CMBS

This acronym stands for "collateralized mortgage-backed securities" and refers to loans that are packaged up and sold to investors on a secondary market. Because of this transfer of ownership, the underwriting is intense and ratios are kept very conservative. Agency loans are a form of CMBS and often have very competitive rates and terms with a tradeoff for prepayment penalties that discourage borrowers from exiting loans early. CMBS are also "non-recourse," making them attractive for individuals with large asset bases they would like to protect and keep separate from their apartment investing.

Banks

Local, regional, and national banks all participate in commercial property lending in some capacity. Some love multifamily and some do not. This feeling often changes with the seasons and who is in charge of a particular credit committee. Overall, sourcing debt from a bank that is local to the market of the asset where you are buying can be an amazing fit. The rates can be very close to CBMS, and the terms are often more flexible. This is the one area of a bank where I do see the relationship side come through. Anything is possible if it passes credit committee. Part of that is because these loans will almost always require a recourse agreement, which means some personal assets are on the line in the event of a default.

Bridge

The ultimate short-term debt product, this is provided by private investors and is sourced through a network of brokers. Investors that have a track record of making big improvements to a property and selling the improved asset within two or three years generally love the bridge loan because it gives them so much flexibility and speed. The LTV on these loans can easily exceed 80% and include cost for construction. However, there is a cost to all these features— the interest rate will be anywhere from 3% to 5% higher than on the stabilized options above. When agency debt is at 5%, bridge will be 8% to 10% and often include more fees as well. Again, these loans only make sense if the investor can create massive value and force appreciation in a small timeframe. These are not loans to be held for the loan's term—they exist for projects and investors that don't have the time or patience to get approval for the stabilized debt options above.

LifeCo

This stands for "life insurance company" loans. Firms like Pacific Life sit on mountains of cash as a result of their business model, and they know commercial real estate is a great asset to provide credit and get consistent returns for their shareholders. These are specialized loans and depend completely on the appetite of independent firms at the time of the ask. We've come close to securing amazing terms through a lifeco loan; however, it was not approved and we pivoted to secure a loan for that deal through agency channels instead.

Seller Financing

Just like it sounds, this is when the seller of a building directly provides the buyer a loan to assist in the purchase. The seller takes the place of the bank. I'm a massive fan and proponent of seller financing. It's rare and unfortunately hard for many people to get their head around, but it makes so much sense. When a seller has significant equity in a building that they sell for a profit, they are in a great position to leave some of that money in and receive monthly interest payments. And for the buyer, these funds are outside of banking and traditional underwriting, so they offer a flexibility that makes them very favorable. And, of course, if the buyer doesn't perform and defaults on the loan, then the seller can take the property back and keep all the equity they've already gained. The inner workings and theory on seller financing could stretch for multiple chapters, so I'll summarize this to say it is a very creative option that I'll pursue in perpetuity.

Other

The list above hits all the major sources of funds, but remember that any two parties can engage in a loan transaction. In fact, private credit notes are formed every day in an "off-market" way between an investor with too much cash and another investor without enough cash. The terms will usually be based on the market terms and adjusted for risk as the lender sees it. I share this point simply to keep your mind open to creative options. Anything is possible here, anything; just align the interests of two parties.

Interest Rate

The most obvious term to know and understand is the interest rate, which is the annual yield charged by the lender for use of its capital. Lenders collect this interest payment monthly, and unless there is a specific carve out, as we'll discuss in a moment, the monthly payment will also include paying down the principal balance.

To take this topic past the obvious for a professional investor in the making, I've learned that interest rates charged to the borrower are made up of two different rates added together. The first is some type of market index, such as the five- or ten-year US Treasury Note (treasuries) or the secured overnight financing rate (SOFR). This will be an objective rate, established by a third party like the Federal Reserve, and will often represent the lender's cost of capital. That's very important because the second input in the interest rate formula is known as a "credit spread." In economics class, we called it a "risk premium." The bank is taking on some risk above their cost of capital; it's their job to price it appropriately. As loans are paid off, they get to keep that spread, it's the profit that motivates a bank to get into commercial lending in the first place.

For apartment loans, the credit spread could be as low as around 100 basis points (1%) or as high as 500 basis points (5%). Add that to a base rate of anywhere from 2% to 10%, and we get quite a huge range in terms of what interest rates could be on an investment loan. Like everything in the capital markets, macroeconomic factors that individual investors have no control over set the interest rates, so it's good practice to make acquisitions that can withstand any credit market cycle.

Term

As mentioned above, most loans for commercial real estate will be five, seven, or ten years. The more profitable and stabilized a property, the longer of a term the lender will be willing to go. Likewise, the more work being done, the more likely the borrower and the lender will want to see the asset with new financing once the work is complete and new leases have been signed at higher numbers.

There is no correct or best term for loans—it all comes down to the business plan. It also comes down to the payment expectations and desires of the lender. Many loans with the lowest rates come with significant prepayment penalties, meaning the lender will enforce the term and not allow early an exit from a loan.

Amortization Period

Different from the term of the loan, an amortization period defines how long it will take to pay the principal of the loan back. As noted above, 25 and 30 years are the most common, but I've seen 20 and 35, and I'm sure there are others. None of these will get the loan repaid in full when the term is shorter, but it does show how fast that principal comes back.

IO Period

Some loans for commercial acquisitions will have a feature called an "interest-only" (IO) period, which is a period of time, usually expressed in months, before the amortization payments kick in. During that time, the borrower only pays the interest each month while the loan balance remains unchanged.

Loans with IO are very popular for value-add and opportunistic investors as they provide more flexibility in the early stage of the project. Some loans issued by agency and life company lenders can feature "full-term IO," which is exactly what it sounds like—only interest payments for the full term of the loan. Its balance will be the same at the end as the beginning. Loans with these features will usually require a highly stabilized asset as collateral to give the bank assurance the borrower will be able to refinance at the end of the loan term.

Common Metrics

In addition to the standard vocabulary above, commercial mortgage bankers have a unique language in terms of how they evaluate deals and describe their offers. Below are the most important of these.

DSCR

This stands for "debt service coverage ratio," and it's a figure that I obsess over when I'm evaluating the financing of an investment. I obsess over it because it's the single most important metric to a lender when analyzing the risk of a loan.

The number is expressed as a decimal number—something like 1.5x or 0.9x. The magic number for most lenders is 1.25x, and that would mean that the property's annual net income is 1.25 times the cost to service the debt being considered. That means the property's operations can fully pay the loan, with a 25% buffer. This implies that the property can suffer declined performance and still comfortably pay back the bank each month. The reason this is significant is that most commercial real estate loans are considered "DSCR-constrained," which means the size of the loan balance is constrained by the DSCR metric.

Let's take a simple example to illustrate both of these points. If a property has a net operating income (NOI) of $125,000 over the trailing 12-month period, then it would qualify for $100,000 of annual debt payments. The size of the loan is then backed into by considering the interest rate and amortization period. If interest rates were 3% and with an amortization of 30 years, then the property could qualify for about $2M in loan proceeds. On the other hand, if interest rates were 7% and the amortization period was 25 years, then loan proceeds would likely not exceed $1.2M. That's a 40% difference! And, as we will show in the next section, it would completely change the return profile of an investment.

A final point on DSCR: not only does it serve as a major tool for sizing a loan and judging its risk; it also follows most loans as a covenant through the life of its term. In other words, the bank will request quarterly financial reports from the borrower, who is responsible to keep the property above a certain DSCR. If the property drops below the mark, the loan would move to a "watchlist," and communication from the lender to borrower would increase dramatically as they apply pressure to correct this metric. Most loan agreements do allow for the bank to take control after violation of DSCR covenants, whether they decide to exert that right is another story.

LTV

This term has been used a few times in the stories above and stands for "loan to value." It's expressed as a percentage, and its formula is (Loan Amount / Property Value = LTV). Just like DSCR, it's a measure of how much debt the property is taking on. However, where DSCR looks from an income perspective and analyzes over a period of time, LTV takes an equity perspective and looks at snapshots in time. DSCR is based on the 12 months trailing or the 12 months ahead. LTV is based on the reality of Tuesday, January 1, 2024, or whatever date is on the calendar when you are doing the analysis.

There is no magic number for LTV in commercial real estate; however, these loans average closer to 65%. There are aggressive bridge lenders that will go 80% or more for distressed properties with a turn-around plan, and there are beautiful assets with ocean views on the California coast that will never qualify for more than 40% LTV. Remember, it's all a function of the amount of income a property produces.

LTC

This stands for "loan to cost" and includes both the purchase price and the approved capital expenditure budget, plus all project fees of a planned acquisition. I think about it as an extension of LTV. Because commercial real estate deals so often include plans to invest capital and improve the site, the purchase price of a deal is only one of two necessary inputs.

In some properties, this is insignificant. In other projects, it's very material. For my first multifamily deal in Riverside, we paid $3.3M and planned for another $1M in renovations and related improvement costs. Adding these two gives a $4.4M true cost for this deal. If the lender provides $2.5M in loan, then the LTV is 76% while the LTC is 57%. This is a sizable difference that can often make or break the return projections for a deal.

Acknowledgments

I'd like to recognize several important people that supported and encouraged me through the process of bringing these ideas to the format of a published book.

First, to my wife, Erin. She's my partner, my best friend, and the person I choose first each day. She is a teacher, a leader, and an inspiration to many. And although she doesn't identify as a real estate investor, she has lived every moment of this journey and has displayed so much courage throughout. It is her calm wisdom that has guided many of the most important decisions documented in these pages.

Next, to my business and investing partner, Greg. His fingerprints are all over the stories in this book—and most of the lessons I share we developed together … during the untold hours we've spent staring through the windshield of a rental car in pursuit of the next acquisition. Our partnership thrives through the mutual obsession with "leveraging each other's strengths."

To Claire and Colin, for their love and patience. One of the greatest gifts of being a parent is having mirrors that follow you around every day. No one else has taught me more about me than these two. And no one else gives me more reason to get up at 4am and put in the work necessary to create something of value for others.

To Katie, Greg's wife, for her trust in me, in us, and this whole "let's buy apartments together" idea in the first place. It takes a village.

To Tom and Leslie, my parents, for 40-plus years of unconditional love, support, and providing an example of life that is worth emulating.

To Bill and Kate, for raising an amazing daughter, inviting me into their family and always encouraging my professional pursuits. "Keep writing!"

To Vance, my mentor and coach, for 20-plus years of asking the same questions and the patience to "honor the journey" and let me find the answers for myself.

To my G-Group, for loving me enough to reframe the question poised on that fateful day. They taught me the difference between "having a book" and "being an author."

To Terrance and Danny, for a high-trust and high-results partnership. As we discovered in San Diego last year, "It's like talking to family."

To my beta readers, for the hours they committed to reading a rough draft of this book and to care enough to provide feedback. The emails I received transformed this work for the better.

Finally, to my entire launch team and anyone who contributed to the spread of these ideas—"above all else, it's the stories that people tell about you because you earn their trust."

About the Author

Dan Reilly is an active real estate investor and entrepreneur. His professional journey is that of employee-to-executive-to-entrepreneur, and this 20-plus year experience provides the foundation for his current investing philosophy.

After earning an advanced degree in business from The University of Southern California, Dan was recruited to join "The Fastest Growing Company in America" in 2005. Finding that he excelled at managing executive-level relationships, Dan left and founded a technology distributor in 2013, a business he profitably exited in 2022.

Since then, he's sponsored the acquisition of eight major private investment deals, including one operating business and seven portfolios of multifamily real estate. Dan loves connecting with investors, putting deals together, and sharing the lessons he is learning along the way.

When he's not figuring out how to buy the next asset or writing his next newsletter, he's a husband, father, and community leader. He lives a few minutes from the beach in sunny Newport Beach and loves the routine of family life.

www.ingramcontent.com/pod-product-compliance
Lightning Source LLC
Chambersburg PA
CBHW050503210326
41521CB00011B/2308